THE JEWISH
ROOTS OF MARY
A Different Look at the Iconic Hebrew Woman

Eli Lizorkin-Eyzenberg

JEWISH STUDIES FOR CHRISTIANS

ISBN: 9798328910057

Contents

Dedication

To Father Alexander Men (1935-1990), an Orthodox Priest of Jewish origin within the Russian Orthodox Church, who was indirectly instrumental in leading me to Christ. He was a true martyr who, at the age of 55, was murdered on the way to his humble church building. His killer was never apprehended. May his voice be loudly heard by God from under the altar of heaven, may he be given a white robe and told to wait just a little while longer. (Rev 6:9-10)

May his memory be blessed!
זכרון לברכה

Acknowledgments

I am grateful to extraordinary people who have contributed to this book by commenting on it and editing portions of my work. I am especially grateful to Jennifer Boudreau, Song Huang, Olga Terekhova, Salvador Talavera, Fr. Dr. David Neuhaus, Arend Warmels, Brian White, Dr. Allen Mawhinney, Fr. Paul Annis, Roberta Currier, Charles Gait, Julia and Victor Blum, Michał Zawadzki, and Dr. Faydra Shapiro.

Their participation in this publication should not be taken as agreement with all or any given point I am making in the book. I also fully acknowledge that I alone assume responsibility for any oversight in the content and any mistakes that may remain.

A Rabbi, a Protestant Minister, and a Catholic Priest
Walk into a neighborhood bar together.

The bartender looks at them and asks: "Is this some
kind of joke?!"

Introduction

Never in my life would I have imagined that the topic of Mary, Mother of Jesus and its relationship with the Jewish tradition (perhaps especially) would pique my interest to such a degree that I would want to commit a considerable amount of time to researching this topic and putting the results of my efforts into writing. But here I am. As they say: Never say never.

For me, as a Jewish follower of Jesus who has received formal theological training and early spiritual formation almost exclusively in Protestant settings, the topic of Mary, Mother of Jesus, was once unthinkable. Even though I long ago departed from "Protestant only" readings by committing to read and learn outside of my normal theological circle, I have never seriously considered the reasoning behind Catholic and Orthodox theology regarding Mary. It seemed so foreign to me that it was out of the question.

Now, I'm compelled to share how I suddenly developed a profound, possibly enduring, interest in Marian studies. It was an unremarkable, rainy day. I was slowly working on my latest book, 'Hebrew Visions of Revelation,' which I co-authored with my long-standing partner and friend, Pinchas Shir, and had just completed writing a segment discussing the Two Witnesses in Revelation 11. Naturally, my focus then shifted to Revelation 12. There, I read:

A great sign appeared in heaven: a woman clothed with the sun, and the moon under her feet, and on her head a crown of twelve stars; and she was pregnant, and she cried out, being in labor and in pain to give birth... And the dragon stood before the woman who was about to give birth so that when she gave birth, he might devour her Child. And she gave birth to a Son, a male, who is going to rule all the nations with a rod of iron; and her Child was caught up to God and to His throne. (Rev 12:1-5)

It was in the process of attempting to provide insightful commentary for my readers when I found myself grappling with a question that seemed both nonsensical and absurd at the time: "Could this possibly be referring to Mary, Mother of Jesus?" The text tells of a woman nearing the birth of a son who was destined to rule all nations with a rod of iron. A dragon was poised to destroy him, but his wicked scheme failed, and the child with his mother escaped. This narrative aligns strikingly with the story of Mary, Mother of Jesus, the one who bore the Messiah. Jesus was the intended victim of a lethal plot by Herod, but his life was spared by a flight into the wilderness, as vividly recounted in the Gospel of Matthew (Matt 2:1-18).

At this juncture in my spiritual journey, I was confronted with a series of unexpected questions: If the figure I suspected (and still do suspect) to be Mary, Mother of Jesus in chapter 12 is elevated to such a prominent position in the Book of Revelation, doesn't this change everything? Could it be that the Christians, who up to this point seemed misguided and ill-informed to me, could be correct about Mary's extraordinary role in God's plan of redemption? Could my long-held belief, instilled throughout my Christian life, that Mary, Mother of Jesus, was a little more than a biblical figure, comparable to the likes of Paul and Peter, be totally off the mark? Could it be that my predominantly Protestant upbringing was akin to growing up in a single-parent family, unaware of a mother who cared, and still cares, for me?

The Jewish Mary in the Gospel of Luke

The Jewishness of Mary

It is very unusual, if not uncomfortable, to think of Mary of Nazareth as an observant Jew. Obviously, today's Orthodox Jewish women would be different from how observant Jewish women looked in the first-century Jewish Galilee. However, they are still the closest modern point of reference we have to be able to place Mary in some context, religious or cultural. We read that Mary and Joseph were careful to observe the Torah:

> [21] And when eight days were completed so that it was time for His circumcision… [22] And when the days for their purification according to the Law of Moses were completed, they brought Him up to Jerusalem to present Him to the Lord [23] (as it is written in the Law of the Lord: "EVERY *FIRSTBORN* MALE THAT OPENS THE WOMB SHALL BE CALLED HOLY TO THE LORD"), [24] and to offer a sacrifice according to what has been stated in the Law of the Lord: "A PAIR OF TURTLEDOVES OR TWO YOUNG DOVES." (Luke 2:21-22)

Two important points stood out for us here. First, the keeping of the period of uncleanness after the birth of Jesus. And second, they went to Jerusalem to do exactly what the Torah said needed to be done in the Temple in order to redeem their firstborn son (see also Luke 2:27). When they came to the Temple to offer Torahprescribed sacrifices, they met Simeon, who picked up Jesus and exclaimed:

> [29] "Now, Lord, You are letting Your bond-servant depart in peace, According to Your word; [30] For my eyes have seen Your salvation, [31] Which You have prepared in the presence of all the peoples: [32] A light for revelation for the Nations, And the glory of Your people Israel." (Luke 2:29-32)

Because both Mary and Joseph were still struggling to grasp what was going on in connection to their son, they were startled by the things that were said about him (Luke 2:33). Addressing Mary, Simeon then said:

> [34] ..."Behold, this Child is appointed for the fall and rise of many in Israel, and as a sign to be opposed— [35] and a sword will pierce your own soul— to the end that thoughts from many hearts may be revealed." (Luke 2:34-35)

Most parents would be satisfied to know that their children will grow up to be decent men and women who take a meaningful part in the life of society around them. This, however, was not Jesus' destiny. Nor was it the destiny of Mary, his mother, who would suffer, together with her son, his torturous death on the Calvary's cross. (John 19:25) The continual Jewish Torah commitments of Mary and Joseph are clear, for we read that "His parents went to Jerusalem every year at the Feast of the Passover." (Luke 2:41). Interestingly, this kind of observance is emphasized by Luke, who, for a supposed gentile, seems to be exceptionally well informed about Jewish religious law and culture (See Appendix II for more on this question). We read:

> [42] And when He was twelve years old, they went up there according to the custom of the feast; [43] and as they were returning, after spending the full number of days required, the boy Jesus stayed behind in Jerusalem, but His parents were unaware of it. (Luke

7

2:42)

The story about the young Jesus' time in the Temple, sharing his ideas with the Jewish priestly elite, amusing them, and making his parents extremely worried is very well known. Finally, they were both relieved and continued to try and make sense of the strange events associated with their son. We read about their anxiety and Mary's words of Jesus,

> [48] When Joseph and Mary saw Him, they were bewildered; and His mother said to Him, "Son, why have You treated us this way? Behold, Your father and I have been anxiously looking for You!" (Luke 2:48)

It was not at all clear to them, neither the events nor Jesus' explanations. We can see that when we read:

> [49] …He said to them, "Why is it that you were looking for Me? Did you not know that I had to be in My Father's house?" [50] And yet they on their part did not understand the statement which He had made to them. (Luke 2:49-50)

Jesus' life between the official beginning of his ministry at around thirty years old and this young age of twelve was a normal and, according to the description, uneventful: "[51] And He went down with them and came to Nazareth, and He continued to be subject to them." (Luke 2:51) Mary again is noted to have "…treasured all these things in her heart. And Jesus kept increasing in wisdom and stature, and in favor with God and people." (Luke 2:51-52)

The Gospel of Luke offers us a glimpse into the lives of Joseph and Mary, who were not just identified as Jews but were also fervently religious. They were devout followers of the Torah of Moses, the central religious text in Judaism, underscoring their deep-rooted faith and commitment to their religion. For Joseph and Mary, the Torah, also known as the Law of Moses, held a revered place in their lives. This was the guiding principle of their existence. It was the foundation upon which they built their lives, and it influenced every decision they made. The text of Luke lays emphasis on the importance they placed on the Torah, demonstrating their unwavering devotion to it.

The Gospel of Luke makes it clear that Joseph and Mary were committed to fulfilling the commandments of the Torah. They didn't merely pay lip service to their faith. They lived it. Their commitment was visible in the way they followed the commandments, not as burdensome rules but as divine guidance for leading a righteous life. They believed in the sanctity and the transformative power of these commandments. The text further reveals that Joseph and Mary had deep faith in the stories told in the Torah. These weren't just ancient tales to them. They were narratives of faith that held profound meaning and relevance in their lives. They believed in the lessons these stories imparted, and they found inspiration and guidance in them. These stories fortified their faith and shaped their worldview.

The Gospel of Luke presents Joseph and Mary as devout Jews for whom the Torah was not just a religious text but a way of life. They were committed to fulfilling its commandments and drew wisdom and guidance from its stories of faith. Their story serves as an inspiring testament to their unwavering faith and dedication to their religious beliefs and practices.

Elizabeth and Sarah

By far, the most extensive and most explicit treatment of Mary in the Bible is found in the Gospel of Luke. Beyond the numerous Marian mentions within the infancy narrative (chapters 1 & 2), Mary's presence is affirmed in Luke 8:19-21, where she is called "mother." An anonymous woman from the masses also acknowledges her in Luke 11:27 by referring to her indirectly, "the womb which bore you [Jesus] and the breasts which nursed you [Jesus]." Because Luke authored the Acts of the Apostles, the final reference to Mary in his works comes in Acts 1:14, where we find the Virgin Mary in the upper room, in company with Jesus' disciples. No other evangelist provides as much Mary material as Luke does. Let us begin with the first several chapters and zoom in on the material there.

After the initial opening and address to Theophilus, the gospel opens with a thoroughly Jewish story involving the Temple, Levites, and righteous behavior as understood within Jewish society. We read:

> [5] In the days of Herod, king of Judea, there was a priest named Zechariah, of the division of Abijah; and he had a wife from the daughters of Aaron, and her name was Elizabeth. [6] They were both righteous in the sight of God, walking blamelessly in all the commandments and requirements of the Lord. [7] And yet they had no child, because Elizabeth was infertile, and they were both advanced in years. (Luke 1:5-7)

The key point here that must not be missed is that Elizabeth and Zechariah very much resemble Abraham and Sarah in their righteousness before God, long struggle with infertility, and the miracle of conception at an advanced age. Mary is reminded of Abraham and Sarah's story and is encouraged through Elizabeth and Zechariah's testimony that God is still the same God. The angel Gabriel appears to both Zechariah and Mary. The only other time Gabriel appears in Scripture is when he is sent to Daniel to help him understand the visions that Daniel was seeing (Dan 8-9). In the Gospel of Luke, we read:

> [8] Now it happened that while he was performing his priestly service before God in the appointed order of his division, [9] according to the custom of the priestly office, he was chosen by lot to enter the temple of the Lord and burn incense. [10] And the whole multitude of the people were in prayer outside at the hour of the incense offering. [11] Now an angel of the Lord appeared to him, standing to the right of the altar of incense. [12] Zechariah was troubled when he saw the angel, and fear gripped him. [13] But the angel said to him, "Do not be afraid, Zechariah, for your prayer has been heard, and your wife Elizabeth will bear you a son, and you shall name him John. [14] You will have joy and

gladness, and many will rejoice over his birth. [15] For he will be great in the sight of the Lord; and he will drink no wine or liquor, and he will be filled with the Holy Spirit while still in his mother's womb. [16] And he will turn many of the sons of Israel back to the Lord their God. [17] And it is he who will go as a forerunner before Him in the spirit and power of Elijah, to turn the hearts of fathers back to their children, and the disobedient to the attitude of the righteous, to make ready a people prepared for the Lord." (Luke 1:8-17)

Once again, I would like to highlight the very Jewish character of the content in this section. The operations of the Jerusalem Temple service are described in detail, which would likely be familiar only to those intimately connected with it (see Luke 1:1-3). Although it is commonly believed that Luke was not a Jew, there is a compelling argument that he indeed was one (read Appendix II).

There are many parallels between the stories of Abraham and Sarah and that of Zechariah and Elizabeth. In the first, Sarah disbelieves the angelic message. In the second, Zechariah is guilty of that. Both times the Lord is firm, but merciful, faithful to his word in the end. We read:

[18] Zechariah said to the angel, "How will I know this? For I am an old man, and my wife is advanced in her years." [19] The angel answered and said to him, "I am Gabriel, who stands in the presence of God, and I was sent to speak to you and to bring you this good news. [20] And behold, you will be silent and unable to speak until the day when these things take place, because you did not believe my words, which will be fulfilled at their proper time." (Luke 1:18-20)

Just as in the story of Abraham and Sarah, a miracle happens, and in due time, the child that will serve the Lord is born. We continue reading:

^{21} And meanwhile the people were waiting for
Zechariah and were wondering at his delay in the
temple. ^{22} But when he came out, he was unable to
speak to them; and they realized that he had seen a
vision in the temple, and he repeatedly made signs to
them, and remained speechless. ^{23} When the days of his
priestly service were concluded, he went back home.
(Luke 1:21-23)

The following text reinforces the intricate connection
between the births of John and Jesus by specifying that Elizabeth
hid her pregnancy from everyone for five long months.

^{24} Now after these days his wife Elizabeth became
pregnant, and she kept herself in seclusion for five
months, saying, ^{25} "This is the way the Lord has dealt
with me in the days when He looked with
favor upon me, to take away my disgrace among
people." (Luke 1:24-25)

Now, the stage is set for Mary of Nazareth to be introduced
to the hearer/reader of the Gospel. This introduction will forever
change the world in a way that no one could have expected. Even
though some other reference anchor could have been given, Luke
ties the time of Gabriel's arrival to speak with Mary to the sixth
month of Elizabeth's pregnancy. We read:

^{26} Now in the sixth month the angel Gabriel was sent
from God to a city in Galilee named Nazareth, ^{27} to a
virgin betrothed to a man whose name was Joseph, of
the descendants of David; and the virgin's name
was Mary. (Luke 1:26-27)

Together with the thoroughly Jewish character of Elizabeth's
life and everything surrounding the events connected with the birth
of John, this extremely familiar text above is also best understood
in its Jewish setting. Gabriel, who is one of the angels serving at
the throne of God Himself, was sent to Mary, probably a teenage,
Jewish girl from a backwoods town of no more than 250 people.

The town may have traced its origins by name to the Messianic hope set forth by the prophets Zechariah and Isaiah (Zech 3:8 and Isa 11:1).[1]

Importance of Hebrew Names

The text will also juxtapose the angel Gabriel speaking to Zechariah with his speaking to Mary. Zechariah, who is found in the very epicenter of God's activity on earth, being both in Jerusalem and in the Temple, disbelieves what he is told. But Mary, a teenage girl from the Jewish Galilean periphery, responds with words of trust, faith, and commitment despite the burden of knowing that she will always be accused of bearing a child out of wedlock.

Take the example of Elizabeth, known in Hebrew as Elisheva, which means "My God is faithful." The New Testament's Elizabeth, mother of John the Baptist, therefore, is reminiscent of the Old Testament's Elisheva, wife of Aaron, the high priest of Israel. This shared name serves as a subtle link, drawing our attention to their shared faithfulness and devotion to God while belonging to the same priestly family.

Mary and Miriam

Here in the Gospel of Luke, Elizabeth is also the wife of Zechariah, the priest. But what about Mary? Does she have an Israelite biblical predecessor? The answer is yes. The older sister of Aaron and Moses was Miriam, but our English translations unjustifiably differentiate Mary and Mariam for us (Ex 15:20).

Do you see how translations, though not purposely, obscure the connections that are intended? Part of it is understandable since we translate the Old Testament from Hebrew, but the New Testament from Greek. This is, regrettably, how connections can be lost if we are not paying close attention. But translators are not

---

[1] This hope was that one day a Messianic servant of Israel will appear. He is referred to symbolically as the Branch. In Hebrew the Branch is *Netser* (נצר), you can see that Nazareth's name in Hebrew is closely related - *Natseret* (נצרת). However, this interpretation is only one possibility among others.

looking out for those things enough to preserve these kinds of parallels either.

We may recall the story surrounding the birth of Moses. After the persecution of the Jews in Egypt, his very survival was in danger. Moses' sister watched with great faith from afar as her baby brother drifted among the reeds in a little basket. His mother, with great sorrow and faith, probably with her older daughter's assistance, had placed him in the basket, entrusting God to safeguard him in the perilous waters of the Nile when she could no longer do so (Ex 2:1-10). Miriam witnessed the saving power of Israel's God firsthand when baby Moses was discovered and adopted into the Egyptian royal family. She never forgot that. How could she? In due course, when Moses led Israel to freedom and emerged safely on the other side of the Red Sea, Miriam led the Israelite women in a jubilant praise and prophetic dance with tambourines (Ex 15:20-21). This was the Mary of the Old Testament. Would the Mary of the New Testament continue in the same tradition of faith, faithfulness, strength, and jubilation? The answer is a resounding - Yes![2] We read about Gabriel's encounter with New Testament Miriam,

> [28] And coming in, he said to her, "Greetings, favored one! The Lord *is* with you." [29] But she was very perplexed at this statement and was pondering what kind of greeting this was. [30] And the angel said to her, "Do not be afraid, Mariam/Mary, for you have found favor with God. (Luke 1:28-30)

If we remember to think of the New Testament Mary as related to the Old Testament Mary, we find the words of Gabriel and Mary's response to them to be far more reasonable and understandable. Just as Miriam/Mary, older sister of Aaron and Moses, was favored to have experienced a great display of God's salvific power, so too the New Testament Miriam/Mary receives God's favor and assurance of God's presence, but in an immeasurably greater way than her predecessor.

---

[2] I am indebted to Fr. Dr. David Neuhaus for this insight.

Mary as Virgin Israel

Just as the Lord gave his promise to Abraham and Sarah, with the two angels visiting their tent in Gen 18:10, he now gives it to Mariam and Joseph. We continue to read in Luke 1:31 - "And behold, you will conceive in your womb and give birth to a son, and you shall name Him Jesus." The issue of Mary's virginity was and still is at the heart of Jewish-Christian disagreement. I will show that even though Jewish and Christian apologists make a huge deal about this and other NT verses that are connected to Isa 7:14, it should not play such a central role in the Jewish-Christian divide. The Hebrew of Isa 7:14 in the Masoretic and other Hebrew texts does not have a virgin, but a young woman. This is the first thing to understand about this controversy.

לָכֵן יִתֵּן אֲדֹנָי הוּא, לָכֶם--אוֹת: הִנֵּה הָעַלְמָה, הָרָה וְיֹלֶדֶת בֵּן,
וְקָרָאת שְׁמוֹ, עִמָּנוּ אֵל

Therefore, the Lord, He will give a sign to you:
Behold, young the woman (הָעַלְמָה) will conceive and birth son, and call his name, "God is with Us"/*Emmanu El* (עִמָּנוּ אֵל). (Isa 7:14, *This literal translation is mine based on the Hebrew text*).

The Septuagint translation that Jewish sages completed from Hebrew into Greek long before New Testament times chose not to translate the Hebrew הָעַלְמָה as "the young woman," but used a Greek word παρθένος, which has a clear, distinct meaning of a "virgin." The Septuagint (LXX) reads as follows,

διὰ τοῦτο δώσει κύριος (Lord) αὐτὸς ὑμῖν σημεῖον
ἰδοὺ ἡ παρθένος (virgin) ἐν γαστρὶ ἕξει καὶ τέξεται
υἱόν καὶ καλέσεις τὸ ὄνομα αὐτοῦ Εμμανουηλ

Because of this, the Lord himself will give you a sign. Behold the virgin in the womb who will conceive and birth a son, and you will call his name Emmanuel. (Isa 7:14, translation from Greek is mine).

15

It is possible that the Jewish translators of Septuagint worked from a different family of Hebrew texts that in fact had Hebrew בתולה, which means virgin. Even though there are cases, in the Dead Sea Scrolls, for example, that show that the Septuagint preserves an older/different version of some Hebrew texts, I think it highly unlikely that this is the case in Isa 7:14. Another far more plausible explanation can be argued.[3] We see that several Hebrew prophets, including Isaiah, routinely referred to God's people Israel as a virgin. Here are but a few examples.

> [13] ... What shall I compare to you, Daughter of
> Jerusalem? What shall I liken to you as I comfort you,
> Virgin daughter of Zion? (Lam 2:13)

> [2] She has fallen, she will not rise again—The virgin
> Israel. She lies unnoticed on her land; There is no one
> to raise her up. (Amos 5:2)

> [21] Then Isaiah the son of Amoz sent word to Hezekiah,
> saying, "This is what the LORD, the God of Israel says:
> 'Because you have prayed to Me about Sennacherib
> king of Assyria, [22] this is the word that the LORD has
> spoken against him: "She has shown contempt for
> you and derided you, The virgin daughter of Zion; The
> daughter of Jerusalem has shaken her head behind you!
> (Isa 37:21-22)

> [4] I will build you again and you will be rebuilt, Virgin
> of Israel! You will take up your tambourines again,
> And go out to the dances of the revelers. (Jer 31:4)

It is possible that Jewish translators of Isaiah were heavily influenced in their translation by Old Testament texts that refer to God's people, Israel, as a virgin. This could have been the reason

---

[3] I am indebted again to my friend and mentor, Fr. Dr. David Neuhaus, for pointing this out to me.

that Luke likely pictured Mary as a symbol of Israel, an ideal representative of God's People, displaying full obedience to her God. This shows that neither the Septuagint's Jewish translators nor New Testament writers themselves were ignorant of the Hebrew text, but that they believed that the original meaning of the Hebrew "young woman" was deeply connected with the "virgin" concept of the Hebrew prophets.

Davidic Kingdom

Gabriel continues to speak with Mary about the kind of son she will give birth to. We continue in Luke 1:32-33:

> He will be great and will be called the Son of the Most High, and the Lord God will give Him the throne of His father David; and He will reign over the house of Jacob forever, and His kingdom will have no end. (Luke 1:32-33)

This phraseology comes directly from Daniel's night visions in 7:13-28. The words of Gabriel are directly connected and fulfill the promise of YHVH given to David through the prophet Nathan in 2 Samuel 7. There we read:

> [12] When your days are finished and you lie down with your fathers, I will raise up your descendant after you, who will come from you, and I will establish his kingdom. [13] He shall build a house for My name, and I will establish the throne of his kingdom forever. [14] I will be a father to him and he will be a son to Me...[15] but My favor shall not depart from him, as I took *it* away from Saul, whom I removed from you. [16] Your house and your kingdom shall endure before Me forever; your throne shall be established forever." [17] In accordance with all these words and all of this vision, so Nathan spoke to David. (2 Sam 7:12-17)

You can see that almost every aspect of Jesus' future mentioned by Gabriel to Mary in Luke 1 is rooted in the promise given to David in 2 Samuel 7. Mary asks an obvious question about these promises of Christ the King being her coming son. She is puzzled how this incredible promise can come true if she has not been physically intimate with Joseph yet. (Luke 1:34). Gabriel answers,

> [35] The angel answered and said to her, "The Holy Spirit will come upon you (ἐπελεύσεται ἐπὶ σέ), and the power of the Most High will overshadow (ἐπισκιάσει) you; for that reason also the holy Child will be called the Son of God. (Luke 1:35)

We will carefully review the Greek language in this verse in chapter I, entitled "Is Mary a New Ark of the Covenant?" to see if a linguistic parallel indeed exists as Catholics argue.

> [34] Then the cloud covered (וַיְכַס הֶעָנָן) the tent of meeting, and the glory of the LORD (וּכְבוֹד יְהוָה) filled the tabernacle. [35] And Moses was not able to enter the tent of meeting because the cloud had settled on it (כִּי־ שָׁכַן עָלָיו הֶעָנָן), and the glory of the LORD filled the tabernacle (וּכְבוֹד יְהוָה, מָלֵא אֶת-הַמִּשְׁכָּן). (Ex. 40:34-35)

Mary's great faith and obedience. As the mother of Jesus Christ, Mary had to navigate unique challenges in giving birth and raising a child without a human father. It is difficult to imagine the extraordinary circumstances she faced. The news from Gabriel likely filled her mind with legitimate fears of condemnation, intimidation, and isolation. She knew she would be subject to scrutiny, judgment, and the potential loss of her reputation. The overwhelming fear of rejection from her community and even her own family must have plagued her thoughts. However, Mary's unwavering faith in the LORD served as her guiding light through the darkest moments. She placed her trust in God's words and found solace in the knowledge that she was part of something far greater than herself. Her strong belief in her child's special mission allowed her to rise above the fears, condemnation, and intimidation she encountered. When Gabriel spoke with her of her coming baby, she said: "How will this be, since I am a virgin?" (Luke 1:34).

Mary's journey as the mother of Jesus is an inspiring example of faith and courage. Despite the challenges she faced, she remained steadfast in her trust in the LORD. Her unwavering faith enabled her to overcome societal pressures and fulfill her divine purpose. Mary's story serves as a reminder that with faith and trust, even the most extraordinary circumstances can be navigated with grace and strength.

We learn that right before Joseph was going to quietly divorce her, an angel came and spoke to Joseph to confirm that what Mary was telling him was the truth. It shows how risky it would have been for Mary to get pregnant without Joseph's involvement. This was not a fairytale; this was life. It was not a given that he would have believed her story. Most probably, he would not have.

The Lord came through for Mary. Her trust in Him was vindicated. We read:

> [18] Now the birth of Jesus the Messiah was as follows: when His mother Mary had been betrothed to Joseph, before they came together, she was found to be pregnant by the Holy Spirit. [19] And her husband Joseph, since he was a righteous man and did not want to disgrace her, planned to send her away secretly. [20] But when he had thought this over, behold, an angel of the Lord appeared to him in a dream, saying, "Joseph, son of David, do not be afraid to take Mary as your wife; for the Child who has been conceived in her is of the Holy Spirit. (Matt 1:18-25)

In response to Mary's objection regarding her virginity, Gabriel says:

> [36] And behold, even your relative Elizabeth herself has conceived a son in her old age, and she who was called infertile is now in her sixth month. [37] For nothing will be impossible with God." (Luke 1:36-37)

The iconic words of a puzzled young Mary, faced with so many things that do not make human sense, will forever be one of the most powerful examples of faith that human beings are capable of. This is why it is right to think of Mary as an ideal and exemplary disciple of Christ Jesus, her Son. We read: "And Mary said, 'Behold, the Lord's servant; may it be done to me according to your word.'" (Luke 1:38) There is a blessing in modern Judaism that no doubt survived centuries if not millennia:

בָּרוּךְ אַתָּה יְיָ, אֱלֹהֵינוּ מֶלֶךְ הָעוֹלָם שֶׁהַכֹּל נִהְיָה בִּדְבָרוֹ

Blessed are You, King of the world, may all will be (according) to your word.

Mary's response lines up with this ancient Hebrew blessing and fits it nearly perfectly, although today, it is mostly used in connection to food and drink. In young Mary's words, there resonates an eloquence of faith, profound in its simplicity. Her readiness to heed the call, her lucid comprehension of God's dominion, and her intimate rapport with the Divine. Her trust is so absolute and unwavering that she relinquishes all reigns of her life, surrendering wholly to His divine orchestration. It's a sentiment of such sublime simplicity and beauty that words can barely capture it in its entirety.

Mary meets Elizabeth

After her meeting with Gabriel, astounded, Mary does the only logical thing she can do. She rushes to see Elizabeth. We read: "When Elizabeth heard Mary's greeting, the baby leaped in her womb, and Elizabeth was filled with the Holy Spirit." (Luke 1:41). The baby noticeably moved in Elizabeth's stomach as soon as Mary walked in, sensing both the presence of Mary and the Incarnate Lord Himself! It is unclear to whom unborn John the Baptist responded to. To Jesus alone or Jesus and Mary? The text does not specify. Elizabeth cried out in surprise at the seeing of Mary - "Blessed are you among women, and blessed is the fruit of your womb!" (Luke 1:42)
What is amazing here is that Elizabeth was not informed by Gabriel that Mary was pregnant. Especially, she was not told that

her cousin Mary would give birth to the long-awaited fulfillment of the promise to King David himself! How did she know? What happened? Before Mary said anything Elizabeth by the leading and the power of the Holy Spirit prophetically announced things that were true, but things that she could not know, except through God's revelation to her.

Blessed among Women

Elizabeth prophetically declared Mary to be: "blessed among women." Later, Jesus will pay tribute to the highly important ministry of his cousin John the Baptist, but it also reflects on Elizabeth because she is his mother: "Truly I say to you, among those born of women there has not arisen anyone greater than John the Baptist!" (Matt 11:11)

What does it mean to be "blessed among women"? It means that among all women that ever lived, not one of them - including Elizabeth - was as honored, privileged, and graced by God as was Mary of Nazareth.

One more caveat should also be given: Elizabeth prophetically announced blessings on both Mary and Jesus all at once. They are declared separate, that's true, but they are declared in one sentence and, more importantly, as one thought (Blessed *are* you among women, and blessed *is* the fruit of your womb!) Later in the Gospel, Luke tempers Mary's greatness, however. In Luke 11, we read about Jesus casting out a demon, which leads to a verbal confrontation with the Pharisees. In the middle of this tense back and forth, we read:

> [27] While Jesus was saying these things, one of the women in the crowd raised her voice and said to Him, "Blessed is the womb that carried You, and the breasts at which You nursed!" [28] But He said, "On the contrary, blessed are those who hear the word of God and follow it." (Luke 11:27-28)

There are a couple of legitimate ways to interpret the mentioned text. Firstly, and the angle some Protestants are accustomed to, positions Mary, the mother of Jesus, in contrast to Christ's true followers. They might explain it like this: While Mary holds a unique position as "blessed among women," there's an even higher level of blessing available. This divine favor is reserved for those who hear and obey the words of Jesus! The big takeaway here is that Mary's blessedness is eclipsed by the blessedness of anyone who hears and obeys the word of Jesus/God. This interpretation resonates well with a Protestant viewpoint.

However, I believe the second interpretation is equally valid (Catholics will obviously like it more). It doesn't set Mary apart from true disciples; instead, it emphasizes the importance of responding to and obeying God's Word, something Mary herself did. For instance, when someone in the crowd says to Jesus, "blessed is the womb that carried You, and the breasts at which You nursed", Jesus redirects their focus. It's not just about the biological act of Mary giving birth and nursing (Luke 11:27), but rather about her complete surrender to God's Word as delivered by the angel Gabriel. Despite her confusion, she humbly responded, "Behold, the bondslave of the Lord; may it be done to me according to your word." (Luke 1:38, also reflected in Luke 2:19).

Elizabeth continued:

> [43] And how has it happened to me that the mother of my Lord would come to me? [44] For behold, when the sound of your greeting reached my ears, the baby leaped in my womb for joy. (Luke 1:43-44)

Elizabeth's words show her amazement that Mary would come to her. It is unclear if Mary herself already understood that she had become pregnant, as the angel Gabriel had promised, without specifying when. Elizabeth confirms that now, before the birth of Jesus, Mary was the mother of her Lord. "And blessed is she who believed that there would be a fulfillment of what had been spoken to her by the Lord." (Luke 1:45). Again, here, Elizabeth displays knowledge that would be available to her only through revelation. She knew something that no one else knew other than Mary.

Mary's Prayer

Mary's exemplary faith, trust, and confidence in God cannot be possibly missed. This is how she prayed (this prayer is known as the Magnificat or Canticle of Mary):

> [46] "My soul exalts the Lord, [47] And my spirit has rejoiced in God my Savior. [48] For He has had regard for the humble state of His bond-servant;
> For behold, from now on all generations will call me blessed. [49] For the Mighty One has done great things for me; And holy is His name. [50] And His mercy is to generation after generation Toward those who fear Him. [51] He has done mighty deeds with His arm; He has scattered those who were proud in the thoughts of their hearts. [52] He has brought down rulers from their thrones, And has exalted those who were humble. [53] He has filled the hungry with good things, And sent the rich away empty-handed. [54] He has given help to His servant Israel, In remembrance of His mercy, [55] Just as He spoke to our fathers, To Abraham and his descendants forever." (Luke 1:46-55)

The 1 Samuel passage serves as a significant reference point for the author of the Gospel of Luke, with several unique parallels emerging. Mary's Magnificat, for instance, is designed to mirror the major themes - and often, the very language - of Hanna's thanksgiving prayer in 1 Samuel 2. Even a brief reading of Hanna's prayer unveils these clear connections.

> [1] "My heart exults in the LORD; My horn is exalted in the LORD, My mouth speaks boldly against my enemies, Because I rejoice in Your salvation. [2] "There is no one holy like the LORD, Indeed, there is no one besides You, Nor is there any rock like our God.
> [3] "Boast no more so very proudly, Do not let arrogance come out of your mouth; For the LORD is a God of

knowledge, And with Him actions are weighed. [4] "The bows of the mighty are shattered, But the feeble gird on strength. [5] "Those who were full hire themselves out for bread, But those who were hungry cease to hunger. Even the barren gives birth to seven, But she who has many children languishes. [6] "The LORD kills and makes alive; He brings down to Sheol and raises up. [7] "The LORD makes poor and rich; He brings low, He also exalts. [8] "He raises the poor from the dust, He lifts the needy from the ash heap To make them sit with nobles, And inherit a seat of honor; For the pillars of the earth are the LORD'S, And He set the world on them. [9] "He keeps the feet of His godly ones, But the wicked ones are silenced in darkness; For not by might shall a man prevail. [10] "Those who contend with the LORD will be shattered; Against them He will thunder in the heavens, The LORD will judge the ends of the earth; And He will give strength to His king, And will exalt the horn of His anointed." (1 Sam 2:1-10)

Both prayers, much like the entirety of the Gospel of Luke and the books of 1 and Samuel, center around the recurring theme of God humbling the proud and uplifting the humble. Mary, for instance, holds an unwavering belief that God will bring humiliation to those who stand against her. Upon reading Mary's prayer in context and comparing it with Hanna's, one can identify numerous instances of a formidable woman who draws her power and assurance from her deep-rooted faith in the divine justice of God. This comparison not only highlights the parallels between the two texts but also underlines the strength and determination of these women in the face of adversity.

In both the Gospel of Luke and 1 and 2 Samuel, the overarching theme of these prayers is the divine principle of humbling the proud and exalting the humble. This theme resonates deeply in Mary's convictions. She harbors an absolute certainty that those who oppose her will inevitably face God's retribution. For example, Hanna prays,

[1] "My heart exults in the LORD; My horn is exalted in the LORD, My mouth speaks boldly against my enemies, Because I rejoice in Your salvation. (2 Sam 2:1)

While Mary prays,

[46] "My soul exalts the Lord, [47] And my spirit has rejoiced in God my Savior. [48] For He has had regard for the humble state of His servant; For behold, from now on all generations will call me blessed. [49] For the Mighty One has done great things for me... (Luke 1:46-49)

In examining Mary's prayer within its context and in relation to Hanna's, one can discern unmistakable examples of a powerful woman who derives her strength and confidence from her unwavering faith in God's justice. This comparison provides a clearer understanding of the parallels between the two scriptures, shedding light on the indomitable spirit and resolve of these women, who stand firm in their faith and trust in divine justice, despite the challenges they face. As Mary prays,

[51b] He has scattered those who were proud in the thoughts of their hearts. [52] He has brought down rulers from their thrones, And has exalted those who were humble. [53] He has filled the hungry with good things, And sent the rich away empty-handed. (Luke 1:51-53)

While Hanna prays,

[7] "The LORD makes poor and rich; He brings low, He also exalts. [8] "He raises the poor from the dust, He lifts the needy from the ash heap To make them sit with nobles, And inherit a seat/throne of honor (2 Sam 2:7-8)

The Birth

Luke 2 reports the census being issued by Caesar Augustus. Joseph and pregnant Mary were residing in Nazareth and had to travel to Bethlehem of Judea, because both were from the house of David. We don't know how long they may have stayed in Bethlehem, although it is unlikely that Joseph traveled with a very pregnant Mary right before his birth. The text simply says while they were there (Luke 2:6) the events later described took place.

Mary and Joseph were probably staying at some relative's place in Bethlehem for a while. Hospitality was highly esteemed by the Jews of the ancient Middle East. To think that somehow no one was willing to welcome a pregnant young lady goes against every Jewish communal value. All families, however, hosting their relatives who came to register for the census were overwhelmed by great numbers of visitors. There were no hotels/inns institutions in the small Judean villages at all. Inns existed but would be located alongside big, important roads only. All hospitality was performed by people, mostly by relatives of relatives and friends of relatives. The translation that says that "there was no room for them in the inn" is simply incorrect (I provide a better translation below).

> [6] While they were there, the time came for her to give birth. [7] And she gave birth to her firstborn son; and she wrapped Him in cloths, and laid Him in a manger (φάτνη), because there was no place for them in the guestroom (κατάλυμα). (Luke 2:6-7)

There is a Greek New Testament word that is translated as inn, but it is not *kataluma* but *pandoxion*, the word that is used in Luke 2:7, for example. We read that Good Samaritan, "came to him and bandaged up his wounds, pouring oil and wine on them; and he put him on his own animal, and brought him to an inn (πανδοχεῖον) and took care of him." The Greek word "kataluma" can be roughly translated as a portion of the house that is used solely for or also for the purpose of hospitality. Relatives of Joseph and Mary overwhelmed that little town and house where Joseph and Mary were already staying. Mary is beginning to have birth pains; she can't imagine giving birth in a room full of people. So, probably with the reluctant advice of the hosts, she relocates to the cave adjacent to the house, which was used by the host family to house animals during the rainy season and was currently empty. It was not much, but it did provide the much-needed privacy.

The Manger

In the luminous narrative crafted by Luke, we witness Mary cradling her newborn child in a manger (Luke 2:7). The nativity scenes often portray this manger as a gleaming crib brimming with straw, yet the truth is far from this. The manger was a feeding trough for humble beasts such as donkeys and oxen, a place far from the immaculate image often depicted. Luke draws attention to the manger not merely to highlight the humble origins of Jesus but to foreshadow the poignant Last Supper. This is the moment where the Messiah offers his body as sustenance for his followers. The manger thus stands as a prophetic symbol, presenting the Jewish Christ to the world and pointing towards his redeeming sacrifice for the salvation of that very world.

Upon the birth of Jesus, Mary tenderly "wrapped him in swaddling clothes and laid him in a manger (φάτνη; phátne)" (Luke 2:7). As the angel of the Lord appears before the shepherds, the divine messenger proclaims, 'For unto you is born this day in the city of David a Savior, who is Messiah the Lord. And this will be a sign for you: you will find a baby wrapped in swaddling clothes and lying in a manger (φάτνη; phátne)'" (Luke 2:12). Stirred by the angel's revelation, the shepherds exclaim, "Let us journey to Bethlehem and witness this miracle that the Lord has revealed to us.' Swiftly, they found Mary and Joseph, and the baby lying in a manger (φάτνη; phátne)" (Luke 2:15-16). The manager, in Luke's narrative, becomes a significant symbol: it is the first earthly cradle that Jesus encounters post his mother's tender embrace, and it serves as a divine "sign" (σημεῖον; semeion) that the shepherds use to identify their Messiah.

Later in the Gospel, Jesus' reference to a manger illuminates its function as an animal feeding trough. Jesus questions the head of a synagogue, "Does not each one of you on the Sabbath untie his ox or his donkey from the manger (φάτνη; phátne) and lead it away to water it?" (Luke 13:15). The fact that

Jesus is laid in this food receptacle at his birth is profoundly fitting, as he is born in Bethlehem (בית לחם; Beit Lechem), which in Hebrew translates to "House of Bread ". This function of the manger foreshadows Jesus' words at the Last Supper: "He took bread (ἄρτος; artos), and when he had given thanks, he broke it and gave it to [the disciples], saying, 'This is my body, which is given for you'" (Luke 22:19).

The infant Jesus resting in a feeding trough comes full circle when he later offers food that symbolizes his own body. Luke, thus, masterfully weaves his Gospel around the imagery of Jesus as "food," symbolizing the joyous promise of salvation for all who partake in him.[4] At the time of their angelic visitation, the shepherds were told that Christ the King was born that he they can easily find him because he will be laying in the manger. When the heavenly delegation departed, they rushed to Bethlehem. We read:

> [16] And they came in a hurry and found their way to Mary and Joseph, and the baby as He lay in the manger. [17] When they had seen Him, they made known the statement which had been told them about this Child. [18] And all who heard it were amazed about the things which were told them by the shepherds. [19] But Mary treasured all these things, pondering them in her heart. (Luke 2:16-19)

Mary experienced a tumultuous year, though the turbulence was predominantly positive in nature, albeit startling. According to the Gospel of Luke, Theophilus was informed that upon hearing the shepherds' testimony, Mary continued to process its significance and possible implications.

---

[4] Schaser J. Nicholas, The Meaning of the Manger. (Israel Bible Weekly, https://weekly.israelbiblecenter.com/the-meaning-of-the-manger)

REQUEST

Dear reader, may I ask you for a favor? If you are enjoying this book, would you take three minutes of your time and provide encouraging feedback to other people about this book? Look up "The Jewish Roots of Mary" on Amazon.com and write a brief review! After that, please drop me a personal note and let me know that you did so - dr.eli.israel@gmail.com. Thank you so much for your support and encouragement!

In His Grace,

Dr. Eli Lizorkin-Eyzenberg

READ HEBREW IN 22 DAYS OR LESS

Jared Abram Seltzer
Eli Lizorkin-Eyzenberg
Pinchas Shir

HEBREW INSIGHTS FROM REVELATION

Eli Lizorkin-Eyzenberg & Pinchas Shir

HEBREW VISIONS OF REVELATION

Eli Lizorkin-Eyzenberg & Pinchas Shir

THE JEWISH ROOTS OF MARY

Eli Lizorkin-Eyzenberg

THE JEWISH GOSPEL OF JOHN

Eli Lizorkin-Eyzenberg

EXPLORE NOW

40 DAYS OF HEBREW DEVOTIONS

Eli Lizorkin-Eyzenberg with Pinchas Shir & Isaac Poceil

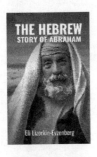

THE HEBREW STORY OF ABRAHAM

Eli Lizorkin-Eyzenberg

THE HEBREW STORY OF JACOB

Eli Lizorkin-Eyzenberg

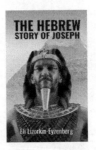

THE HEBREW STORY OF JOSEPH

Eli Lizorkin-Eyzenberg

THE Samaritan WOMAN RECONSIDERED

Eli Lizorkin-Eyzenberg

INSPIRATIONAL INSIGHTS ABOUT LIFE

Eli Lizorkin-Eyzenberg & Oren Lizorkin

70 DAILY HEBREW MUSINGS

Eli Lizorkin-Eyzenberg & Yeshaya Gruber

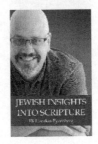

JEWISH INSIGHTS INTO SCRIPTURE

Eli Lizorkin-Eyzenberg

THE JEWISH APOSTLE PAUL

Eli Lizorkin-Eyzenberg

Can Mary Really Pray for Us?

I'd like to share a humorous anecdote I came across, originally told by a Russian Jewish stand-up comedian, Gary Guberman. The joke unfolds as a conversation between two elderly friends, Abram and Chaim. Abram, who is 87 years old, decides to visit his older friend, Chaim, who is 97.

Abram: "Chaim, I came to say goodbye because tomorrow I will be departing this life. I've lived a long and happy life, but now I'm ready to go, and for sure this will happen tomorrow."

Surprised by his younger friend's certainty, Chaim has a peculiar request.

Chaim: "Abram, I have a favor to ask of you."
Abram: "Yes, Chaim. Anything."

Chaim: "Tomorrow, when you go, you'll get to a better place and at some point in there, you may meet the Creator, Blessed be He. It is possible that He will ask you about me. So, please, tell him that you have not seen me for a while and have no idea where I am."

Communion of Saints

Putting humor a side, how should we look at those who have departed from this earth? Are they dead? Does the fact that their expected resurrection did not yet take place justify us calling them so? Or are they are alive? If so, how?

We see this very clearly when we read Jesus' answer to the Sadducees. In one of their interactions with the Messiah, they posed a trick question to Jesus about what happens to the remarried wife of several brothers within the context of levirate marriage after the resurrection of the dead (a doctrine that Sadducees themselves rejected, but Jesus affirmed). We read in Matthew:

> [29] But Jesus answered and said to them, "You are mistaken, since you do not understand the Scriptures nor the power of God... [31] ...regarding the resurrection of the dead, have you not read what was spoken to you by God: [32] 'I AM THE GOD OF ABRAHAM, THE GOD OF ISAAC, AND THE GOD OF JACOB'? He is not the God of the dead, but of the living." (Matt 22:29-32)

Jesus is saying rather clearly that Abraham, Isaac and Jacob, despite the occurrence of their physical deaths on earth, are in fact very much alive in the presence of the Lord, since He is being referred to in the Hebrew Bible/Old Testament as the God of Abraham, Isaac and Jacob (Ex 3:15). The Lord is not the God of the dead, but of the living.

Returning to my personal journey, I long ago concluded that there is absolutely nothing wrong with asking God's people who have left this earth and are now in the presence of God in heaven to continue to pray for us. This is no less legitimate than asking people here on earth to pray for us. For example, if I can ask you, my dear reader, to intercede for me, there is nothing wrong in my asking someone who is now with the Lord to do the same. One might say it makes even more sense.

The Apostle's Creed enshrined this idea into the very fabric of emergent Christianity. There we read, particularly in the final paragraph:

> I believe in God, the Father almighty, creator of heaven and earth.
> I believe in Jesus Christ, his only Son, our Lord,
> who was conceived by the Holy Spirit
> and born of the virgin Mary.
> He suffered under Pontius Pilate,
> was crucified, died, and was buried;

he descended to hell.
The third day he rose again from the dead.
He ascended to heaven
and is seated at the right hand of God the Father almighty
From there he will come to judge the living and the dead.
I believe in the Holy Spirit,
the holy universal church,
the communion of saints,
the forgiveness of sins,
the resurrection of the body,
and the life everlasting. Amen.

Did you notice that as early as the Apostle's Creed, which is recognized by all Christian movements, Catholic, Protestant, and Orthodox, early Christians believed that they were not alone in this world? After all, they publicly confessed that they believed in the "communion of the saints." So instead of "praying *to* the saints" we should think instead about "praying *with* the saints." Even though many today understand "communion of saints" as having to do with believers who are currently on earth, historically this was understood as active fellowship with all true believers, both those who presently walk the earth and those who are continuing their journey in heaven. The Book of Hebrews captures some of this sentiment. We read,

[32] And what more shall I say? For time will fail me if I
tell of Gideon, Barak, Samson, Jephthah, of David
and Samuel and the prophets, [33] who by
faith conquered kingdoms, performed *acts*
of righteousness, obtained promises, shut the mouths of
lions, [34] quenched the power of fire, escaped the edge
of the sword, from weakness were made strong,
became mighty in war, put foreign armies to flight.
[35] Women received *back* their dead by resurrection;
and others were tortured, not accepting their release, so
that they might obtain a better resurrection; [36] and
others experienced mocking and flogging, and further,
chains and imprisonment. [37] They were stoned, they
were sawn in two, they were tempted, they were put to

death with the sword; they went about in sheepskins, in
goatskins, being destitute, afflicted, tormented
[38] (*people* of whom the world was not worthy),
wandering in deserts, *on* mountains, and *sheltering*
in caves and holes in the ground... [12:1] Therefore, since
we also have such a great cloud of witnesses
surrounding us, let's rid ourselves of every obstacle
and the sin which so easily entangles us, and let's run
with endurance the race that is set before us, [2] looking
only at Jesus, the originator and perfecter of the faith,
who for the joy set before Him endured the cross,
despising the shame, and has sat down at the right hand
of the throne of God. (Heb 11:1-38-12:2)

Of course, some important objections that will be brought up
by our Protestant brothers and sisters will need to be answered.
One of them will surely have to do with Moses' prohibition against
inquiring of the dead.

Prohibition against Consulting the Dead

The objection is brought up by some Protestant brothers
and sisters is based on Deuteronomy 18:

[10] There shall not be found among you anyone who
makes his son or his daughter pass through the fire,
one who uses divination, a soothsayer, one who
interprets omens, or a sorcerer, [11] or one who casts a
spell, or a medium, or a spiritist, or one who consults
the dead. [12] For whoever does these things is detestable
to the LORD; and because of these detestable things
the LORD your God is going to drive them out before
you. [13] You are to be blameless before the LORD your
God. [14] For these nations, which you are going to
dispossess, listen to soothsayers and diviners, but as
for you, the LORD your God has not allowed you to
do so. [15] "The LORD your God will raise up for you a
prophet like me from among you, from your
countrymen; to him you shall listen." (Deut 18:10-15)

The text above needs to be read carefully. In fact, there is nothing in this text which prohibits all contact with those in the afterlife. Even Christ Jesus, who kept the Law of Moses perfectly, communicated with the departed from this world when Moses and Elijah appeared to support his mission at the Transfiguration. (Matt 17:3).

The Deuteronomy 18 text does not forbid requesting intercessory prayer from God's people who are in heaven but rather forbids seeking from them information, insights, and wisdom about life's challenges. The text specifies that the people of Israel must instead draw their spiritual direction from the prophetic ministry of Moses-like prophets that God will provide. In other words, wisdom can only come from the Word of the Lord. Wisdom cannot come, or at least must not be sought, from those who have gone on.

In other words, we should differentiate between the forbidden act of conducting a spiritualist seance as described in Deuteronomy 18:10-15, which is a truly pagan thing to do, and the humble request for prayerful intercession, as would be the case with asking Mary, Mother of Jesus for intercession. Even though for most Catholic Christians this sounds like an unfathomable and even preposterous connection/accusation, some Protestant brothers and sisters see them as connected, and they deserve a good answer.

The precise nature of Deuteronomy's prohibition can be clearly seen in a very interesting text found in 1 Sam 28, one that puzzles many readers but, perhaps, in the context of our discussion, will make good sense.

Saul Consults Samuel

In 1 Samuel the Philistines had gathered their armed forces to fight the Israelites. The prophet Samuel had died, and Saul had actively removed all mediums and spiritists from the land. It was a great and God-honoring reform. King Saul gathers Israel's forces as well. He was terrified (1 Sam 28:3-5). Saul then inquired of the Lord, but the Lord delayed in answering him by all three of the possible ways: dreams, *urim* and *tumim*, or by the word of the prophets. Instead of waiting upon the Lord Saul urgently commissioned his servants to find a certain woman-medium (1 Sam 28:6-7) who was once famous for her accomplishments in the fortune-telling business. King Saul and two of his trusted men went incognito to her home and requested her evil services.

> [8] "Consult the spirit for me, please, and bring up for me *the one* whom I shall name for you." [9] But the woman said to him, "Behold, you know what Saul has done, that he has eliminated the mediums and spiritists from the land. Why are you then setting a trap for my life, to bring about my death?" [10] So Saul swore an oath to her by the LORD, saying, "As the LORD lives, no punishment shall come upon you for this thing." [11] Then the woman said, "Whom shall I bring up for you?" And he said, "Bring up Samuel for me." (1 Sam 28:8-11)

The big lesson to be taken from the above text is that Saul specifies precisely why he has come to the medium – "to consult the spirit." Later, he will specify to Samuel why he has asked for his presence. Only after the medium has initiated the contact at the request of her mysterious guest does she recognize him as Saul. Naturally, she was afraid, but it was too late. Samuel has come to speak with the living. When Saul recognizes Samuel as the one appearing before them, he falls face to the ground and pays homage to him (1 Sam 28:12-14). The most important thing here is to recognize that the Bible understands that the living can, in fact, communicate with those who have passed away. Even though the story from 1 Samuel describes a truly sinful request by Saul, the fact of such human ability cannot be denied.

The problem with raising 1 Sam 28 as an objection to asking for saints to pray for us is that Saul did not want the prophet Samuel to pray for him. His reason for meeting Samuel was different. He sought insight/knowledge that would help him to know how to defeat his enemies. In other words, Saul was literally consulting with the dead. Next, we read:

> [15] And Samuel said to Saul, "Why have you disturbed me by bringing me up?" Saul replied, "I am very distressed, for

the Philistines are waging war against me, and God has abandoned me and no longer answers me, either through prophets or in dreams; therefore, I have called you, so that you may let me know what I should do." (1 Sam 28:15)

Saul is led by fear, impatience, and lack of faith in the goodness of the Lord towards his people ("God has abandoned me and no longer answers me, either through prophets or in dreams"). Samuel then challenges Saul about the logic of coming to the prophet of the Lord if it was indeed true that the Lord had abandoned him and became his enemy. He then confirms to Saul that the time will soon come when he will no longer be king, and the kingdom will pass to David (1 Sam 28:16-19).

In the preceding discourse, my argument posits that the prohibition in Deuteronomy is not a blanket ban on all interactions with those in the afterlife. Instead, it specifically discourages soliciting guidance for life's predicaments from them. Deuteronomy 18 distinctly advocates for seeking spiritual enlightenment only from God's prophets. It further suggests displaying patience, even if it entails waiting indefinitely to hear their prophecies. The crux of the matter lies in discerning the difference between engaging in spiritualist séances — a practice explicitly condemned in Deuteronomy 18 and associated with Saul's actions — and soliciting prayerful intercession. This latter act is a common practice among tens of millions of Catholic, Orthodox, certain Lutheran, and Anglican Christians, who request those who have gone ahead to be with the Lord to intercede for them.

Lazarus and Abraham

There is a fascinating story told by Jesus in the Gospel of Luke, which can shed some light on how at least some Jews understood the accessibility of believers such as Lazarus, who went to the same place as Abraham, presumably Heaven.

> [19] "Now there was a rich man, and he habitually dressed in purple and fine linen, enjoying himself in splendor every day. [20] And a poor man named

Lazarus was laid at his gate, covered with sores, [21] and longing to be fed from the scraps which fell from the rich man's table; not only that, the dogs also were coming and licking his sores. [22] Now it happened that the poor man died and was carried away by the angels to Abraham's arms; and the rich man also died and was buried. [23] And in Hades he raised his eyes, being in torment, and saw Abraham far away and Lazarus in his arms. [24] And he cried out and said, 'Father Abraham, have mercy on me and send Lazarus, so that he may dip the tip of his finger in water and cool off my tongue, for I am in agony in this flame.' [25] But Abraham said, 'Child, remember that during your life you received your good things, and likewise Lazarus bad things; but now he is being comforted here, and you are in agony. [26] And besides all this, between us and you a great chasm has been set, so that those who want to go over from here to you will not be able, nor will any people cross over from there to us.' [27] And he said, 'Then I request of you, father, that you send him to my father's house— [28] for I have five brothers—in order that he may warn them, so that they will not come to this place of torment as well.' [29] But Abraham said, 'They have Moses and the Prophets; let them hear them.' [30] But he said, 'No, father Abraham, but if someone goes to them from the dead, they will repent!' [31] But he said to him, 'If they do not listen to Moses and the Prophets, they will not be persuaded even if someone rises from the dead." (Luke 16 19-20)

The limitation of using Luke 16:19-31 as evidence that departed believers can be or should be contacted for help is straightforward: it is a parable. The purpose of this parable is not to teach Jesus' disciples that departed believers can hear and assist, but rather to emphasize the sufficiency of the Word of God, represented by Moses and the Prophets. The parable suggests that miracles are not what instills faith in people; it is the Word of God that holds the power to do so. Therefore, if the Word of God does not evoke faith, miracles will not either.

Consequently, it is misguided to use this parable to argue for seeking help from departed believers. However, this parable does tell us that the Jews of Jesus' time and Jesus the Jew himself may have believed, together with many later Jews, that the departed righteous can indeed be asked to intercede/pray for those who are still living on earth. In the above example, we see that the Bible itself neither commends nor forbids the idea of requesting people who have gone. This whole discussion is recognizable very protestant and I understand that and as those among my dear readers who are Catholics to be kind to the rest us.

Requesting Prayer from the Departed in Rabbinic Judaism

It may come as a surprise, especially to many Protestant Christians, but Jewish tradition has a well-established idea about prayer at the gravesites of righteous Jews. This tradition believes that the prayer of a living petitioner may gain strength to reach the heavenly throne due to the merits of the righteous person buried in that place. Alternatively, it is believed that the righteous person buried there can be asked to pray or intercede for something or someone on earth. For example, the Talmud recounts the story of Caleb, one of the spies sent to explore the Holy Land, who visited the Cave of the Patriarchs in Hebron. Rabbis speculate about why he did it. We read:

> It is also stated with regard to the spies: "And they went up into the south, and he came to Hebron" (Numbers 13:22). Why is the phrase "and he came" written in the singular form? The verse should have said: And they came. Rava says: This teaches that Caleb separated himself from the counsel of the other spies (מְלַמֵּד שֶׁפֵּירֵשׁ כָּלֵב מֵעֲצַת מְרַגְּלִים) and went and prostrated himself on the graves of the forefathers (הָלַךְ, וְנִשְׁתַּטַּח עַל קִבְרֵי אָבוֹת). He said to them: My forefathers (אֲבוֹתַי!), pray for mercy for me (בַּקְּשׁוּ עָלַי רַחֲמִים) so that I will be saved from the counsel of the spies. (Sotah 34b)

The rabbis opined here that he prostrated himself before the cave and implored his forefathers to intercede on his behalf, seeking protection from the spies' evil intentions. Additionally, the Talmud mentions a custom of visiting cemeteries during times of calamity, such as drought, with the belief that the deceased will beseech mercy for humanity in Heaven. We read:

> Why do they go out to the cemetery (לְבֵית הַקְּבָרוֹת)?
> Again, Rabbi Levi bar Ḥama and Rabbi Ḥanina
> disagree with regard to this matter. One said this is as
> though to say: We are like the dead before You. And
> one said that one goes out to the cemetery in order that
> the deceased will request mercy on our behalf (כְּדֵי
> שֶׁיְּבַקְשׁוּ עָלֵינוּ מֵתִים רַחֲמִים). (Taanit 16a)

In other words, two rabbis disagree. Rabbi Levi bar Ḥama says the reason Jews have an ancient custom to pray at the cemetery is so that their mortality can be remembered. Rabbi Ḥanina has a wholly different idea in mind – they go there to ask departed righteous Jews to intercede for mercy upon the living. Throughout history, it has been a Jewish tradition to regard the graves of the righteous (*kivrei tzaddikim*) as places of pilgrimage, where Psalms and prayers are recited.

Hassidim, a subset of ultra-orthodox Jews, for example, leave notes (*kvitlach*) at the graves of their spiritual rabbinical leaders. Not only that, but in Judaism, worshipers routinely engage in conversation with angelic beings through prayers and songs. For example, in prayer *Machnisei Rachamim,* Jewish congregants pray the following:

> Angels of mercies (מַכְנִיסֵי רַחֲמִים), put our mercies
> (הַכְנִיסוּ רַחֲמֵינוּ) Before the Lord of mercies (לִפְנֵי בַּעַל
> הָרַחֲמִים) Propagators of prayer (מַשְׁמִיעֵי תְּפִלָּה), make our
> prayer heard (הַשְׁמִיעוּ תְּפִלָּתֵנוּ) Before the Hearer of
> prayer (לִפְנֵי שׁוֹמֵעַ תְּפִלָּה) Propagators of cries (מַשְׁמִיעֵי
> צְעָקָה), make our cry heard Before the Hearer of cries
> (לִפְנֵי שׁוֹמֵעַ צְעָקָה) Presenters of tears (מַכְנִיסֵי דִמְעָה), put
> our tears Before the King who gives in to those in tears
> (לִפְנֵי מֶלֶךְ מִתְרַצֶּה בִּדְמָעוֹת) Do your best (הִשְׁתַּדְּלוּ) and lift

up prayer. Lift up prayer and supplication (וְהַרְבּוּ תְּחִנָּה
וּבַקָּשָׁה) Before the King high and exalted (לִפְנֵי מֶלֶךְ אֵל
רָם וְנִשָּׂא)

In other words, Judaism treats requests to departed righteous Jews in the same exact way it treats requests to heavenly angels to strengthen the prayers of the Jews and to take them up to God.[5]

Rachel as Israel's Intercessor

A more direct and positive Scriptural indication that the saints of old do, in fact, intercede for others who still live on earth may be found in Jeremiah. Rachel was Jacob's favorite wife, a biblical figure known for the extensive suffering endured. Long after Rachel's death, Jeremiah claims that when Rachel sees Israel's exiles departing Jerusalem, she weeps for them and that God, in fact, hears her voice. We read:

[15] This is what the LORD says: "A voice is heard in Ramah, Lamenting and bitter weeping. Rachel is weeping for her children; She refuses to be comforted for her children, Because they are no more." (Jer 31:15)

Naturally, it is possible to interpret Jeremiah as speaking poetically rather than literally. We can't be sure. However, if Jeremiah meant what he wrote literally, then this is a very important text. We will discuss this text in considerable detail later because it is possible that Mary, Mother of Jesus, is presented in the Gospels as a new Mother Rachel, a powerful intercessor for the people of Israel.

---

[5] It appears that in both cases, Judaism, while open to it as can be seen above, exercises an abundance of caution to avoid guilt of idolatry. This can be observed from cautionary and at times even condemnatory statements about both practices by ancient and modern Jews who oppose this practice (Mishna Berurah 559:41, 581:27).

Christis is Not the Only Intercessor

The second serious hesitation that a Protestant Christian would have about approaching saints in heaven to intercede for the living (which would include asking for intercessory prayer from Mary, Mother of Jesus) is that Scripture clearly states there is no mediator between God and humanity other than Jesus. (1 Tim 2:5-6) A great example that shows that believers above in fact do actively pray about earthly affairs is found in Revelation, chapter 6:

> [9] ...I saw underneath the altar the souls of those who had been killed because of the word of God, and because of the testimony which they had maintained; [10] and they cried out with a loud voice, saying, "How long, O Lord, holy and true, will You refrain from judging and avenging our blood on those who live on the earth?" (Rev 6:9-10)

What is this prayer if not a request to expedite justice on behalf of the suffering Christ-followers who still live on earth by those who now live in heaven? Prayer intercession by fellow believers, be it on earth or in heaven, evidently does not impede Christ's singular role as a mediator. This is further supported by the four verses preceding 1 Timothy 2:5 (For there is one God, and one mediator also between God and mankind, the man Christ Jesus), when Paul encourages believers to intercede for one another in prayer, stating:

> First of all, then, I urge that entreaties and prayers, petitions, and thanksgivings be made on behalf of all men, for kings and all who are in authority, so that we may lead a tranquil and quiet life in all godliness and dignity. This is good and acceptable in the sight of God our Savior, who desires all men to be saved and to come to the accurate knowledge of the truth. (1 Tim. 2:1-4)

Therefore, it is evident that intercessory prayers made by the followers of Christ for others, whether on this earth or already in heaven, are good and acceptable in the sight of God and do not encroach in any way on Christ's unique, mediatory role. He is indeed the only mediator between God and humanity.

No Explicit Biblical teaching

Another objection that our brothers and sisters from the Protestant church will have concerns the fact that there is no explicit teaching in the Bible about this. This objection, like others, should not be brushed off lightly but instead addressed so that we, as brothers and sisters in the Lord, may seek God's light on this matter.

First, it is true that, to my knowledge, there is no explicit commandment in the Old and New Testaments for believers to request prayerful intersession from those who have left this earth. But that does not mean that there is a prohibition to do so. Consider, for example, the following: We have already seen that the saints in heaven pray. In fact, they pray quite passionately and actively (Rev 5:8; Rev 8:3-4; Rev 6:10). We have also seen that some Old Testament figures, such as Rachel — wife of Jacob and one of the mothers of Israel — prayed to God in such a way that he heard and recognized her prayer about Israel's exiles long after she departed the earth (Jer. 31:15). While there does not seem to be a direct commandment or teaching that believers ought to request intercessory prayers from other believers in heaven, implicitly, there is enough scriptural evidence to show that such a request is not completely illegitimate.

Second, there are many examples of doctrines and practices that have been accepted by all Christian denominations, including Protestants, yet they lack direct or explicit teaching from the Bible. Take, for example, the doctrine of the Trinity. As you well know, the word Trinity is not in the Bible. Moreover, the Christian doctrine of the Trinity is not formulated explicitly in Scripture. It took Christian believers some time to recognize that its basic ideas are, in fact, correct. In other words, something that was there in the Bible in an implicit way was discovered and accepted by Christians in time. The same goes for other doctrines that require systematization and aggregation of many biblical texts into a coherent summary.

The condemnation of slavery is another good example. It took the Church a long time to realize that this evil does not have a right to exist in a society impacted by the Word of the Living God. However, while the Bible sets a trajectory that will eventually lead Christians to the abolition of slavery, it is precisely that: a trajectory rather than an explicit teaching. Yet today all Christian denominations fully support the abolition of slavery. There is no discussion about this topic. The case is closed, and rightly so.

Monogamy is yet another topic, and the Bible is not at all clear about it. No laws or directives for monogamy are set forth, only trajectories. Polygamy is explicitly forbidden only when it comes to the elders of the church (1 Tim 3:1-2). Nothing of this sort is specified for all believers. This is yet another example of something that is right, even though it was not explicitly taught in the Bible.

Third, numerous Jewish books were made into the Catholic and Orthodox bibles, but these are not found in the Protestant version. You can look up the full list, it is rather large. Among these missing books are the Books of Maccabees. The now world-famous story of Chanukkah comes to us from there. We read about Jesus' celebration of Chanukah (in English, the Feast of Dedication) in the Gospel of John (John 10:22-23).

In 2 Maccabees we read a very interesting text that builds upon something that we already mentioned in discussing Jeremiah's views of Rachel's intercession before God on behalf of Israel:

[12] In his vision, Judas (Judah) saw Onias, who had been high priest and was virtuous, good, modest in all things, gentle of manners, and well-spoken. From childhood he had learned all things that properly belong to a good moral life. This man had his hands extended to pray for the entire nation of the Jews. [13] Then in the same manner, another man, noteworthy for his gray hair and dignity, appeared with astonishing and splendid glory. [14] Onias said, "This

man is one who loves his brothers and sisters and prays many prayers for the people and the holy city: God's prophet Jeremiah." (2 Mac 15:12-15)

Judah the Maccabee sees a vision in which Jeremiah, the prophet appears, and his special intercessory role is both acknowledged and highlighted. He is with the Lord in heaven, yet he loves to pray for his brothers and sisters who are still on earth. This text shows that it is disingenuous for protestants to say that something is not found in the Bible, when what they really mean that it is not found in the Protestant Bible.

A common myth, however, often arises, suggesting that the Catholic Church added books to the Bible. The canon of the Church, determined at the Council of Rome in 382, included 46 books in the Old Testament and 27 in the New Testament. This decision was reaffirmed by subsequent councils at Hippo (393), Carthage (397, 419), II Nicea (787), Florence (1442), and Trent (1546). Furthermore, the allegation that the Catholic Church introduced these deuterocanonical books in 1546 becomes untenable when we realize that these books were already included in Martin Luther's first German translation, which was published prior to the Council of Trent. In addition, these books were present in the inaugural King James Version (1611) and the very first Printed Bible, the Gutenberg Bible, which predates the Council of Trent by a century.

In fact, these books were a standard inclusion in nearly all versions of the Bible until 1825, when the Edinburgh Committee of the British Foreign Bible Society decided to remove them. Until that point, even if not part of the main Bible text, these books were at least included in the Protestant Bibles as a kind of "suggested reading," which Luther himself considered "books which are not considered equal to the Holy Scriptures but are useful and good to read."

Is Mary Really a New Rachel?

As background information throughout this book, I will engage with Catholic scholar Brant Pitre's "Jesus and the Jewish Roots of Mary" (2018). While I agree with many aspects of his work, I also take exception to his methodology, approach, reasoning and certainly conclusions in many places. Nevertheless, I recommend reading Pitre's book alongside mine as it will enhance your experience reading this book. Probably the most interesting chapter in his book is the one that seeks to recast Mary as a Catholic version of Jewish Rachel. It is very interesting on the one hand and very problematic on the other. But you of course be the judge. This why after all your are reading this book – so that you can make up your own mind.

Merits of the Fathers

Perhaps counterintuitively, I want to start this discussion by talking about a famous Jewish concept "the merits of the fathers". Soon, you will know why.

The basic concept here has to do with extraordinary actions of the fathers of Israel – Abraham, Isaac, and Jacob. The "merits of the fathers" refer the righteous deeds of the original covenant members. These merits produce very positive outcomes for the descendants of Israel. The idea that the righteous Christ Jesus can obtain salvation for sinners by his sacrifice on the cross is the ultimate expression of *this* ancient Jewish concept.

Judging from Jewish liturgical practices the sacrifice of Isaac by Abraham is the ultimate righteous deed in Torah (Gen 22). Abraham displays ultimate faith in being willing to put his only son Isaac to death in obeying YHVH. It becomes an example of the highest display of trust, that all future generations of Israelites still derive spiritual benefits from. The children of Israel, as members of the covenant, receive these extraordinary benefits because "the merits of the fathers" are always remembered by YHVH and are treasured by Him. We see this idea very clearly already in Genesis when God speaks to Isaac about the merits of his father, Abraham. We read:

> [24] And the LORD appeared to him the same night and said, "I am the God of your father Abraham; Do not fear, for I am with you. I will bless you and multiply your descendants, For the sake of My servant Abraham." (Gen 26:24)

Moreover, this concept is also found in the Amida, the central Jewish prayer that in other contexts is simply called *tefilah* (prayer). It is composed of 19 blessings and the very first one remembers the "merits of the fathers". We read:

בָּרוּךְ אַתָּה יְהֹוָה אֱלֹהֵינוּ וֵאלֹהֵי אֲבוֹתֵינוּ אֱלֹהֵי אַבְרָהָם אֱלֹהֵי יִצְחָק
וֵאלֹהֵי יַעֲקֹב הָאֵל הַגָּדוֹל הַגִּבּוֹר וְהַנּוֹרָא אֵל עֶלְיוֹן גּוֹמֵל חֲסָדִים טוֹבִים
וְקוֹנֵה הַכֹּל וְזוֹכֵר חַסְדֵי אָבוֹת וּמֵבִיא גוֹאֵל לִבְנֵי בְנֵיהֶם לְמַעַן שְׁמוֹ
בְּאַהֲבָה

Blessed are You, LORD, our God, and God of our fathers, God of Abraham, God of Isaac, and God of Jacob, the Almighty, the Great, the Powerful, the Awesome, most high Almighty, Who bestows beneficent kindness, Who possesses everything, Who remembers the pious faithfulness of the fathers, and Who brings a redeemer to their children's children, for the sake of His Name, with love.

מֶלֶךְ עוֹזֵר וּמוֹשִׁיעַ וּמָגֵן: בָּרוּךְ אַתָּה יְהֹוָה מָגֵן אַבְרָהָם

King, Helper, Deliverer, and Shield. Blessed are You, LORD, Shield of Abraham.

In Judaism, the concept of the "merits of the fathers" is a very important idea that, in many ways, constitutes the very basis of a covenantal relationship with God. It certainly is of such importance as to be listed first among 19 topics. This ancient Jewish idea is clearly visible in the letter to the Romans. In fact, Paul's letters are one of the earliest witnesses to this idea. There, speaking about Jews who did not accept the Messiahship of Jesus and played a part in opposing his cause, he writes, "In relation to the gospel they are enemies on your account, but in relation to God's choice they are beloved on account of the fathers." (Rom 11:28) According to the Apostle Paul, even their rejection of Jesus does not disqualify Jews as beloved by Israel's God on account of the fathers Abraham, Isaac, and Jacob. This is an unbelievable statement indeed.

Rachel's Suffering and Tragic Life

Jews around the world follow a system of reading through the Hebrew Bible as laid out and organized by the rabbis long ago. In it, portions of the Torah (Five Books of Moses) are paired up with various selected readings from the Hebrew prophets. What is interesting is that on the Rosh Hashana holiday, the reading of Genesis 22, telling of Abraham's offering Isaac on the altar, is paired with a reading from the prophet Jeremiah 31 that includes Rachel weeping for Israelite exiles. This, in Jewish liturgical tradition, sets up Rachel as a kind of female counterpart of Abraham.

Rachel's life is truly full of suffering and tragedy. It all starts with meeting Jacob when he arrives in Padan Aram, fleeing the conflict with his brother Esau. Not long after, Jacob asks Laban to give his beautiful young daughter Rachel to him in marriage. Laban agrees but asks Jacob to work for him for seven years before marrying her. Upon the completion of the seven-year term, Laban switches Leah with Rachel, and Jacob unknowingly into Leah instead of Rachel, only to discover this trickery in the morning. In ancient times, having sexual intercourse with someone was equivalent to marrying that person. Imagine the emotional state of Rachel, who is supposed to become Jacob's wife but is cheated by her own father from this joy and honor. Sometime in the same week, Laban gives Rachel to Jacob as advance pay for seven more years of work. Rachel becomes Jacob's second wife.

To add insult to injury, God blesses Leah with children when he sees that she is loved less than Rachel. But like Sarah and Rebekah before her, Rachel has trouble conceiving. Eventually, Rachel conceives a son and calls him Joseph. Joseph's life before his eventual exaltation is even more tragic. And given any mother's connection to her child, Joseph's sufferings naturally add to the tragedy of Rachel's own life.

To make a truly long story short, some of Joseph's half-brothers want to kill him, but he ends up in Egyptian slavery instead. From the Bible, it is not entirely clear whether Rachel was still alive when Joseph's tragic events unfolded. On the one hand, Genesis 35:18 speaks about the tragic death of Rachel at the birth of Benjamin, Joseph's full brother. Joseph has his famous dreams and relates them to his brothers only in Genesis 37. So, the obvious presumption is that since chapter 35 comes before chapter 37, then Rachel already gave birth to Benjamin and died before Joseph is sold to Egyptian slavery. This also may explain why Jacob made for teenage Joseph a flashy tunic, setting him apart from his older siblings from other mothers. Jacob may have thought he was honoring the departed Rachel this way.

On the other hand, something doesn't quite work here, and it is possible that the stories relating to Joseph and Rachel are not told chronologically (this is not the first time this would happen in the Bible). Jacob challenges his son after he hears about the second dream with the following: "What is this dream that you have had? Am I and your mother and your brothers actually going to come to bow down to the ground before you?" (Gen 37:10b)

This reads as if Rachel were still alive. Genesis 37 may be a story flashing back in time. Genesis is known for telling stories twice. Also, when a very old Jacob reunites with his son Joseph, who rose to immense power in Egypt, Jacob feels it is important to recount to him how and where his mother died as if Joseph was not aware of it. "Now, as for me, when I came from Paddan, Rachel died, to my sorrow, in the land of Canaan on the journey when there was still some distance to go to Ephrath. I buried her there on the way to Ephrath (that is, Bethlehem)." (Gen 48:7)

On the other hand, this may not be the exact words of Jacob since it is not Jacob but Moses who is much later penning down for Israel, as what happened in the past. Also, they are told in the context of Jacob telling Joseph that he will adopt his two sons, who were born to him in Egypt. So, it is possible that Jacob is not so much as informing Joseph (after all, Joseph would have asked about his mother much earlier in the story), but recalling this tragic event and arguing his case.

There are many other arguments for and against the idea that Rachel died before Joseph's slavery in Egypt. The case does not appear to be settled. If Rachel had been alive when Joseph disappeared, imagine the intense suffering she must have endured when the brothers brought Joseph's shredded clothes, covered in blood. In this scenario, Rachel dies, never knowing what really happened. She most likely constantly relived in her dreams the wild animals attacking and carrying away the lifeless body of her beloved son. She dies without realizing how God, through Joseph and the murderous intent of his brothers, was in fact bringing salvation to the whole family of Jacob.

Before she died, however, God, in his mercy, gave Rachel another son. Jacob rightly names him Benjamin (the son of my right hand) even though Rachel wants to call him Ben Oni (the son of my sorrow). Rachel realizes that while she has succeeded in giving him life, she will not survive this ordeal. Rachel died that day, giving Jacob another son and another brother to Joseph. Her loving husband Jacob buries her in the vicinity of Bethlehem. We read. "So Rachel died and was buried on the way to Ephrath (that is, Bethlehem)." (Gen 35:19)

In death, Rachel is further singled out for the ultimate separation, for she is buried not with her husband or her ancestors, but on the road, away from everyone else. This reinforces the sense of profound suffering that relates to Rachel in Jewish memory. On the other hand, if Rachel died before Joseph's slavery it could be argued that she still had plenty of undeserved suffering in her life even without knowing of Joseph's slavery. She can be considered the greatest woman of suffering featured in the Torah.

If Jeremiah was not speaking only poetically and really believed that Rachel was weeping for the sons of Israel marching in shackles into exile via the road by Rachel's grave, then surely her dying before Joseph's slavery did not stop her from knowing about it and agonizing from the other side of life either.

The Power of Rachel's Prayer

In later Rabbinic material, the plot thickens. We read in Genesis Rabah the question: "What was Jacob's reason for burying Rachel on the way to Ephrat?" Evoking Jer 31:14-15, the midrash answers that "Jacob foresaw that the exiles would pass on from there. Therefore, he buried her there so that she might pray for mercy for them. (Gen Rab 82:10) As was mentioned in the previous chapter, long after Rachel's death, Jeremiah declares that when Rachel sees Israel's exiles departing Jerusalem, she weeps for them, and that God then hears her voice of intercession. We read:

> [15] This is what the LORD says: "A voice is heard in Ramah, Lamenting and bitter weeping. Rachel is weeping for her children; She refuses to be comforted for her children Because they are no more." (Jer 31:15)

Rachel is the ancestress of the Northern Kingdom, which was named Ephraim after Joseph's son. After Ephraim and Benjamin are exiled by the Assyrians, Rachel is remembered as the classic mother who mourns and intercedes for her children. Rachel's centrality within the concept of "merits of the fathers/mothers" appears in the midrash, which preserves a rabbinic debate about identifying the tribe to which the prophet Elijah belongs. Rabbi Eleazar argues that Elijah belongs to the tribe of Benjamin, while Rabbi Nehorai counters that he belongs to the tribe of Gad. We read:

> These names are meant for allegorical interpretation: when [God] would shake the world, Elijah recalls the merit of the ancestors ... On one occasion our Rabbis were debating about Elijah, some maintaining that he belonged to the tribe of Gad, others, to the tribe of Benjamin. Whereupon he came and stood before them

and said, 'Sirs, why do you debate about me? I am a descendent of Rachel.' (Gen Rab 71:9)

Rachel is repeatedly portrayed in Jewish religious poems as praying to God. The rabbinic midrashim present Rachel as an eternal mother of the people of Israel whose barrenness, untimely death, accumulation of merit due to several episodes of loss and self-sacrifice, and her timeless supplications in later generations can intervene in God's judgment of her descendants. They transform Rachel not only into a heavenly maternal intercessor but the most meritorious matriarch, whose merit transcends generations.[6]

We now come to the best example by far of how Rachel becomes the most powerful intercessor in Judaism. Even though Judaism knows four mothers of Israel, Rachel is the one who takes the leading role. We read in Lamentations Rabah that:

> Rabbi Shmuel bar Naḥman said: When the Temple was destroyed, Abraham came before the Holy One blessed be He weeping, pulling out his beard, tearing out the hair of his head, striking his face, rending his garments, ashes on his head, and he was walking in the Temple and lamenting and screaming... 'Master of the universe: Why did You exile my children, deliver them into the hand of the nations, kill them with all kinds of uncommon deaths, and destroy the Temple, the place where I elevated my son Isaac as a burnt offering before You?' (Lam Rab, Petichta 24)

This text shows the emotional level of engagement by Father Abraham when it comes to interceding for Israel's children in exile. He doesn't just sympathize, he suffers. The exiles are not some remote needy people. They are his posterity, his very flesh and blood, in dire straits. The midrash describes this passionate, imagined, and ultimately failed address of Abraham to God.

---

[6] Gribetz, Sarit Kattan. "Zekhut Imahot: Mothers, Fathers, and Ancestral Merit in Rabbinic Sources." *Journal for the Study of Judaism in the Persian, Hellenistic, and Roman Period* 49, no. 2 (2018): 280. https://www.jstor.org/stable/26551249.

The God of Israel gives his reasons for rejecting Abraham's plea for mercy and help. The story moves on to Isaac intervening for the children of Israel, where he makes a claim about his merits before the Almighty and pleads for Israel. But he, too, receives a negative answer from God. Then Jacob intercedes and addresses God, but Jacob, too, is unsuccessful in his intercession. Now, it is Moses' turn. Moses begins and says,

> 'Master of the universe, was I not a loyal shepherd
> over Israel for forty years? I ran before them like a
> horse in the wilderness, yet when the time came for
> them to enter the land, You decreed against me that my
> bones would fall in the wilderness. Now that they have
> been exiled you sent to me to lament them and weep
> over them.' (Lam Rab Petichta 24)

God is apparently unimpressed. Moses fails as well. The midrash then recounts that Moses is in conversation with the prophet Jeremiah. Together, they reach the rivers of Babylon, where Israel's exiles are situated. The exiles, Moses and the Bat Kol (divine voice) interact with each other, and the exiles then raise passionate prayers of their own. When Moses encounters Abraham, Isaac, and Jacob and talks with them about Israel's exiles, he tells them of the children of Israel suffering in Babylonian captivity. The fathers of Israel begin profusely weeping and lamenting. Then something unexpected happens.

Rachel — the text calls her "our matriarch" — interjects her appeal. She recounts her life of suffering, especially regarding Laban's night of "bait and switch" tactics. She appeals to her ability to take her own jealousy under control and argues from lesser to the greater. If she could do it, can't God do it too? If she forgave and blessed Leah, the Midrashic storyteller, who takes some liberties from the original text, couldn't God forgive and bless Israel too? We read:

> If I, who is flesh and blood, was not jealous of my
> rival, and I did not lead her to humiliation and shame,
> You who are a living and eternal merciful King, why
> were You jealous of idol worship that has no

substance, and You exiled my descendants, and they were killed by sword, and the enemies did to them as they pleased? (Lam Rab Petichta 24)

What happens next, given the intercessory failures of Abraham, Isaac, Jacob, and Moses, is unprecedented:

> Immediately, the mercy of the Holy One blessed be He was aroused, and He said: 'For you, Rachel, I will restore Israel to its place.' That is what is written: "So said the Lord: A voice is heard in Rama, wailing, bitter weeping. Rachel is weeping for her children; she refuses to be consoled for her children, as they are not" (Jeremiah 31:14). And it is written: "So said the Lord: Restrain your voice from weeping, and your eyes from tears, as there is reward for your actions.... And there is hope for your future, the utterance of the Lord, and your children will return to their borders" (Jeremiah 31:15–16) (Lam Rab Petichta 24)

The point here is not that the Midrashic storyteller has additional information that is missing from the Torah but that in Jewish minds, Rachel continues to emerge as the supreme intercessor for the children of Israel.[7]

Mary as New Rachel

So far, we have seen that the ancient Jewish idea of the "merits of the fathers" includes not only the fathers but also the mothers of the faith. We have seen how, in Judaism, a particular woman has earned a very special place of becoming the chief intercessor for the people of Israel. Her name is Rachel, and she has earned that reputation because among all women and certainly among all the foremothers of the nation of Israel, the suffering and tragedy that she bore was unique.

---

[7] Sivan, H. (2019). Rachel Weeps in Ramah: Of All the Patriarchs, God Listens Only to Her. (www.thetorah.com)

Moreover, the key biblical text around which all speculation and religious imagination spirals is Jeremiah 31:15, where the prophet declares that even though Rachel has died, she somehow continues to intercede for the exiled children of Israel in such a powerful way that her voice is heard by Israel's God loud and clear.

The Gospel of Matthew, in its very beginning, tells the story of Jesus' birth and early survival. This is rather a famous story told and retold so many times that there is no reason to repeat it here. Thus, I will pick up my discussion from a particular point in this story: when Herod learns there is a good chance that in a little town known as Bethlehem, someone is born who one day may be Israel's king (Matt 2:1-2). Upon hearing this, Herod acts decisively and ruthlessly.

One key point to understand is that Bethlehem is not only very close to Jerusalem, but it has been rumored among some to be the future birthplace of Christ, Israel's King. Had the birthplace of Jesus been somewhere other than Bethlehem, or perhaps at least not in Judea, Herod might not have been so worried. The name Bethlehem raises a red flag in Herod's mind, and his suspicion is confirmed by spiritual advisers, who have the wisdom he sought on this matter (Matt 2:4-6).

Because the magi – a caste of highly educated men from some distant Eastern country who specialized in astronomy, astrology, and natural science – claim that they have seen his star, Herod becomes paranoid, as would anyone who is desperate to hold on to power. He understands that anything the people perceive to be of heavenly origin will not survive any level of government control.

Herod does not believe for a second that Christ, the long-awaited King of Israel, had just been born in Bethlehem. Yet he knows that if the story of the Magi from the East gets out, with its perfect makings of a legend, this will fuel Messianic speculation, which could put either him or his appointee/descendant out of royal business. Herod authorizes a mass murder of all children under two years old, just to be sure, born in the vicinity of Bethlehem to put his fears to rest. We read in Matthew:

Then what had been spoken through Jeremiah the

prophet was fulfilled: A voice was heard in Ramah, weeping and great mourning. Rachel weeping for her children. And she refused to be comforted because they were no more. (Matt 2:17-18)

The angel of the Lord appears to Joseph and instructs him to evacuate Mary and Jesus from the province of Judea and take them all the way to the land of Egypt. This is the first time that Rachel's intersession from Jer. 31:15 is somehow connected with what is directly happening to Mary in Matthew 2.

Brant Pitre brilliantly combines his Catholic commitments together with research in Jewish studies. He has passionately and capably popularized what people before him have already said - Mary is the New Testament equivalent of the Old Testament Rachel. In his book *Jesus and the Jewish Roots of Mary*, Brant Pitre suggests three connections between Mary and Rachel:

First, the massacre of the infants happens in the vicinity of Rachel's tomb. Mary gives birth practically next to Rachel's tomb (Bethlehem). Second, Rachel's intercession is explicitly quoted in Matthew 2:17-18. So, the author of the Gospel of Matthew clearly thinks that there is a connection. Third, both Rachel and Mary suffer because of the identity and the purpose of God in the lives of their sons Joseph and Jesus, respectively.[8] Brant Pitre quotes David Flusser, one of the late pioneers of the Jewish Jesus research from the Hebrew University of Jerusalem:

"In Matthew, Rachel is a symbolic figure for the suffering mother, in this case, the suffering Jewish mother. And Rachel's pain for the dead children is also symbolic for the suffering of Mary in relation to her illustrious son."[9]

He also quotes Jacob Neusner, arguably the most prolific Jewish scholar of the recent past, as confirming that the Catholic Mary should be seen in connection with the Jewish Rachel:

---

[8] Pitre, Brant James. Jesus and the Jewish Roots of Mary (p. 183). The Crown Publishing Group. Kindle Edition.

[9] Flusser, Pelikan, and Lang, Mary: Images of the Mother of Jesus, 11-12.

"That is why I can find in Mary a Christian, a Catholic Rachel, whose prayers count when the prayers of great men, fathers of the world, fall to the ground... No wonder that when Rachel weeps, God listens. How hard, then, can it be for me to find in Mary that sympathetic, special friend that Catholics have known for 2,000 years! Not so hard at all. So, yes, if Rachel, then why not Mary?"[10]

Brant Pitre writes:

"Indeed, on a very human level, it is easy to imagine Mary weeping not only for the persecution and exile of her own son, but for the lives of all the boys who were massacred in the attempt to kill her child."[11]

My own take

What do I think about all of this?! Well... Although I am a sympathetic reader of Brant Pitre's work, I am not persuaded just yet that Pitre, Flusser, and Neusner are right about the kind of connection they see between Matthew 2 and Jeremiah 31. So far, what we can verifiably deduce from Matthew 2 is that Rachel, Israel's matriarch, was very much engaged in intercession not only for the Jewish people who were exiled to Babylon but also for the Jewish boys murdered by Herod's kill squad in the time of infant Jesus. Whether or not Mary is portrayed there as the New Testament equivalent of Old Testament Rachel cannot be deduced from chapter 2 of Matthew's Gospel.

I am open to seeing if further evidence, not based solely on Matthew's quotation of Jeremiah 31, will show the connection between Mary and Rachel as Old Testament/New Testament counterparts. But for now, at least to me, the connection is not yet certain.

As compelling as Brant Pitre's quotations and the

---

[10] Neusner, "Can People Who Believe in Different Religions Talk Together?," 99 in Pitre, Brant James. Jesus and the Jewish Roots of Mary (p. 227). The Crown Publishing Group. Kindle Edition.
[11] Pitre, Brant James. Jesus and the Jewish Roots of Mary (p. 171). The Crown Publishing Group. Kindle Edition.

arguments are, I remain open but unpersuaded.

Please allow me to take a brief pause on the discussion of the Jewish Roots of Mary and turn your attention to the discussion of the Jewish Jesus to explain my problems with Pitre's arguments here. In the Gospel of Matthew, Jesus gives a teaching that becomes known in history as the "golden rule." [12] So whatever you wish that others would do to you, do also to them, for this is the Law and the Prophets. (Matt 7:12). Rabbi Hillel, whom Rabbinic Jewish texts place living a few centuries before Jesus, is remembered to have said: "What is hateful to you, do not do to your neighbor. That is the whole Torah; the rest is the explanation of this - go and study it!" (Shabbat 31a)

The basis of each text is an effort to summarize the entire Torah, encompassing hundreds of positive commandments (*mitzvot aseh),* and negative commandments (*mitzvot lo taaseh*) in one basic principle. Both men give the same answer, but Jesus states it positively (telling us what *to do*), and Hillel states it negatively (telling us what *not* to do). Ultimately, however, it boils down to one and the same idea.

Yet, we should still ask: How do we know that Jesus said this, and when did he say it? We know he said it because it is recorded in the Gospels, and we know that the Gospels were written sometime in the first century. But how do we know that Hillel said what he said? We know this because the statement is preserved in the Talmud. This means that the document from which we draw the identity of the person to whom the "golden rule" is first attributed was written down/codified/authored at least 400 years after Jesus! Do you see the problem? Yes, Hillel lived more than 100 years before Jesus, but the saying is attributed to Hillel 400 years after Jesus's events.

In this case, could it not also be that Jesus is the original author of the "golden rule," but because Jewish followers of Jesus were heavily integrated into the rest of Jewish society, this idea may have been accepted into non-Messianic Judaism through them? One can almost imagine a discussion of early rabbis debating:

"Do not do unto others what is hateful to you who could have said that?" "This does not sound like Shammai;

perhaps it was Hillel?" "Yes, most likely. Let's attribute this saying to him."

No doubt, this imagined discussion may not have taken place. The idea, though, that Hillel was the original author of the "golden rule" may indeed be correct. However, given the problem with our sources, this could have gone either way.

Yet, another interpretive option exists here that both Hilel and Jesus arrived at their conclusions independently, because they were basing them upon the same Holy Scriptures! After all they both drank from the same deep well of ancient Jewish tradition. At this point, you may be thinking, "Interesting, but what does it have to do with our discussion about Mary and Judaism?". But don't you see? It has *everything* to do with it.

The problem is that all the fabulous quotations from the Jewish tradition that Brant Pitre's cited, in comparison to the Gospels, are very late sources. Moreover, could a plausible conclusion then be that the Jewish sources referred to above testify to the practice that emerged in Judaism much later in response to Marian exaltation in Christian theology?

In other words, the identity of Rachel as an intercessor may have in fact been influenced by Mariology, and thus wasn't documented until later. Such possibilities testify that late Jewish sources have very limited value in interpreting early Jewish sources (such as the New Testament). We should then only rely on the Jewish sources that come before or roughly contemporary to Jesus events.

The same goes for the quotations from those two Jewish studies heavyweights - Flusser and Neusner. They, too, rightly draw beautiful parallels between the Jewish ideas of Rachel, the great matriarch of Israel and a powerful intercessor, and Mary, Mother of Jesus and all Christians, the great intercessor of the faithful, as understood and believed by Catholic Christians worldwide. There is no question that Jewish Rachel and Christian Mary have much in common, but do they have it already in the New Testament times? Or, perhaps, the Church first developed Marian theology over the first three centuries, which in turn resulted in Jewish theology countering with the Rachel alternative later. The answer is yes. This means that it is good to know about the possible connection between Rachel, Israel's matriarch, and Mary, the matriarch of the Church, but for now, it should remain just that, a beautiful but only possible connection.

REQUEST

Dear reader, may I ask you for a favor? If you are enjoying this book, would you take three minutes of your time and provide encouraging feedback to other people about this book? Look up "The Jewish Roots of Mary" on Amazon.com and write a brief review! After that, please drop me a personal note and let me know that you did so - dr.eli.israel@gmail.com. Thank you so much for your support and encouragement!

In His Grace,

Dr. Eli Lizorkin-Eyzenberg

Is Mary Really a New Eve?

Seeming Disrespect

This study, in some ways, helps me to relive my younger days when I was living in Odessa, Ukraine, back in 1990. It was *Perestroika* time in the former Soviet Union. Everything looked new, and the sense of discovery was bright and vivid. This was a time when I was willing to examine things that lay completely outside of my normal worldview.

I remember first reading the story of the Wedding in Cana in the Gospel of John. This is the first miracle of Jesus, where he turns water into wine, saving a beautiful young couple and their parents from terrible embarrassment when the kitchen runs out of wine (John 2:1-11). However, one of the things that struck me back then was how Jesus interacted with his own mother. I have been asked this question many times, and I am sure you, too, dear reader, have found yourself wondering about the same. We read in John's Gospel:

> [1] On the third day there was a wedding in Cana of Galilee, and the mother of Jesus was there; [2] and both Jesus and His disciples were invited to the wedding. [3] When the wine ran out, the mother of Jesus said to Him, "They have no wine." [4] And Jesus said to her, "What to me and to you, woman (Τί ἐμοὶ καὶ σοί, γύναι)? My hour has not yet come." His mother said to the servants, "Whatever He tells you, do it." (John 2:1-5)

Jesus' mother, brothers/cousins, and his disciples are among many people invited to the wedding (John 2:1, 12). When the wine runs out, Jesus' mother turns to him and says: "They have no wine." Jesus' answer seemed so odd to me in my early days of exploring the New Testament. Not only does his response seem to display an attitude of not caring for the needs of others, but what is more, he addresses his mother as a 'woman.' This seems like a highly offensive and disrespectful way to speak to one's mother, so I intuitively knew back then that I was missing something that both Jesus and his beloved mother must have known. After all, her response is a positive one. She tells the waiters to follow Jesus' coming instructions. Also, Jesus listened to her request and came through for the people in need.

There is only one other instance in the New Testament where Jesus addresses his mother again as "woman." It is also found in the Gospel of John when an eyewitness describes Jesus' suffering on the cross. There at the foot of the cross stand three Marys, the beloved disciple,[12] and perhaps, though we cannot be sure about it, others who are unnamed. We read:

---

[12] The identity of the "Beloved Disciple" in John's Gospel has been the subject of extensive theological debate. Some of the main interpretations include John the son of Zebedee (John the Apostle), Lazarus, Mary Magdalene, an unknown/ unnamed member of Jerusalem's priestly elite and James, brother of Jesus. That Jesus would entrust his widowed mother to the care of John son of Zebedee is not surprising since John was Jesus' cousin, although why Jesus entrusted John to Mary is another important question. The familial bonds were significant. Another interpretation posits that "beloved disciple" is simply a literary device used to point to all followers of Jesus loved by Him in all generations. The phrase "the disciple whom Jesus loved" (ὁ μαθητὴς ὃν ἠγάπα ὁ Ἰησοῦς), or as depicted in John 20:2, "the other disciple whom Jesus loved" (τὸν ἄλλον μαθητὴν ὃν ἐφίλει ὁ Ἰησοῦς), is a distinct expression that appears in the Gospel of John six times. Uniquely, this phrase does not emerge in any other New Testament narratives recounting the life and teachings of Jesus. This phrase is not only a witness to the intimate relationship between Jesus and the disciple but also signifies the depth and purity of divine love embodied by Jesus. I tend to think that the use of the phrase is to tell the story, not to single out one disciple, but to highlight the message of divine love as universal and reaching out to all individuals. Like most scholars, I don't know for sure who the beloved disciple is. My hunch, especially in the context of the above discussion, is that the language of the "beloved disciple" may point to the connection of every single beloved follower of Christ as entrusted into Mary's care at the foot of the cross. In this reading, all God's people are his beloved disciples. This may be the reason why the identity of this person was kept secret for all generations.

^{25} … But standing by the cross of Jesus were His mother, and His mother's sister, Mary the wife of Clopas, and Mary Magdalene. ^{26} When Jesus then saw His mother, and the disciple whom He loved standing nearby, He said to His mother, "Woman, behold, your son!" ^{27} Then He said to the disciple, "Behold, your mother!" From that hour the disciple took her into his own household. ^{28} After this, Jesus, knowing that all things had already been accomplished, to fulfill the Scripture, said, "I am thirsty." (John 19:25-28)

While suffering the excruciating pain of crucifixion following prior beatings and extraordinary exhaustion from carrying his cross, Jesus sees his beloved mother standing right next to him at the foot of the cross. She is sobbing, being comforted, and no doubt held back by the two other Mariams/Marys. Jesus first addresses his mother: "Woman, behold your son" (Γύναι, ἴδε ὁ υἱός σου). He then addresses the beloved disciple: "Behold, your mother" ("Ἴδε ἡ μήτηρ σου).

We must temper our possible excitement, however, because these are the only two times that Jesus addresses his mother at all in the entire Bible. Therefore, we must be careful not to infer too much from this. Moreover, Jesus calls "woman" other women he meets as well: Matt 15:28 (a Canaanite woman), Luke 13:12 (a crippled woman in the Synagogue), John 4:21, 8:10 (a Samaritan woman). Angels address Mary Magdalene at Jesus' resurrection in the same way (John 20:13). At no point does this seem to be a disrespectful reference. Having said that, while there is nothing strange in Jesus' calling other women "woman," it does sound very strange for him to address his own mother in this way.

My friend, mentor, and former New Testament professor Dr. Allen Mawhinney pointed out to me that the note in Liddell and Scott's Greek-English Lexicon reminds us that the vocative of γυνή can be used as "a term of respect or affection." The Liddell and Scott Greek-English Lexicon is renowned as the foundational text for all serious scholarship from the classical period onward, often referred to as the "granddaddy" of all Greek lexicons. (Incidentally, both authors were Anglicans with a robust commitment to Marian veneration). [13]

But why, if Jesus' words contained no hint of insult, did he choose "woman" instead of "mother"? Most likely, as John explicitly states, the moment at Cana signified the initiation of Jesus' "signs," his messianic signs, thus marking the onset of his public messianic ministry. Thus, his choice of words is not an insult but a clear signal that from that day on, their relationship was to be irrevocably transformed. With his messianic destiny about to be revealed publicly, Mary's relationship to Jesus was set to evolve beyond the intimate familial bond they had shared for years. Although she was the one who gave birth to him and raised him, at the wedding in Cana, a pivotal change in their relationship was imminent.

Why did he still call her "woman" in the very end of his earthly ministry? We will soon find out.

First Woman

We can clearly see now that there is no way Jesus' address of his mother as "woman" indicates any sign of disrespect. For now, suffice it to say that this is the context within which Jesus, for the second time, addresses his honorable and beloved mother as a woman. I will present evidence that may lead us toward the conclusion that John's Gospel makes a strong connection between Mary, Mother of Jesus and the very first woman known as Eve. It is interesting that Eve is mentioned by name only twice in the Book of Genesis (Gen 3:20; 4:1), while the text refers to her as "woman" ten times (Gen 2:22, 23; 3:1, 2, 4, 6, 12, 13, 15, 16). For example, we read that Adam calls his companion woman:

וַיֹּאמֶר הָאָדָם זֹאת הַפַּעַם עֶצֶם מֵעֲצָמַי וּבָשָׂר מִבְּשָׂרִי לְזֹאת
יִקָּרֵא אִשָּׁה כִּי מֵאִישׁ לֻקֳחָה־זֹּאת׃

---

[13] Liddell, Henry George, Robert Scott, and Henry Stuart Jones. *A Greek-English Lexicon*. 9th ed. with revised supplement. Oxford: Clarendon, 1996.

καὶ εἶπεν Ἀδάμ Τοῦτο νῦν ὀστοῦν ἐκ τῶν ὀστέων μου καὶ σάρξ ἐκ τῆς σαρκός μου· αὕτη κληθήσεται Γυνή, ὅτι ἐκ τοῦ ἀνδρὸς αὐτῆς ἐλήμφθη αὕτη.

23 Then the man said, "At last this is bone of my bones, And flesh of my flesh; She shall be called 'woman,' (אִשָּׁה; Γυνή) Because she was taken out of man." (Gen 2:23)

The Hebrew word for Eve is חַוָּה (hava), which means she who gives life, while the Hebrew word for woman is אִשָּׁה (isha), and its basic meaning connects with such concepts as humanity, weakness and fragility. Jewish scholars, translating the Hebrew Bible into Greek, translate the word אִשָּׁה (isha) to the Greek word Γυνή (guney). It is the same word that the Gospel of John has Jesus using in addressing his mother: "What to me and to you, woman (Τί ἐμοὶ καὶ σοί, γύναι)? and "Woman, behold your son" (Γύναι, ἴδε ὁ υἱός σου).

However, Mary may relate to Eve beyond Jesus' calling his mother "woman" twice in the same gospel, although this is still very significant. Perhaps we can also find a hint in the Hebrew meaning of the word Eve and how it can be connected to the matter of wine as a Judaic symbol of life. As I already mentioned, the Hebrew word behind the English Eve is חַוָּה (hava). Its basic meaning is "life-giver". This is the same root for the famous Hebrew word חיים (hayim), which means "life". When Jewish scholars translated the Torah into Greek, they communicated this very clearly. For example, in Gen 3:20 we read:

וַיִּקְרָא הָאָדָם שֵׁם אִשְׁתּוֹ חַוָּה כִּי הִוא הָיְתָה אֵם כָּל־חָי׃

Καὶ ἐκάλεσεν Ἀδὰμ τὸ ὄνομα τῆς γυναικὸς (אִשְׁתּוֹ; his woman/wife) Ζωή (חַוָּה; Eve), ὅτι αὕτη μήτηρ πάντων τῶν ζώντων.

Now the man, called his woman's name Eve (*Zoe*), because she was the mother of all the living. (Gen 3:20)

In the Bible Hebrew names given to individuals are not given to them randomly, rather there was always some kind of meaning to the names. Here too we see from the above quote that Eve/Hava/Zoe is the name that communicates the idea of giving of life. The Greek word the Jewish scholars used to translate Hava/Eve (חַוָּה) was Zoe (Ζωή). There are several different English words that are derived from this Greek word, such as zoology, which is the branch of biology that studies animal life.

If Mary is indeed portrayed in John's Gospel as a second Eve given John 2 and John 19 references cited above, then it is reasonable to expect that there would be more connections. Let us now examine a possible connection that may exist in John's Gospel but one that often escapes our attention because we are reading the text in English and not in its original languages.

Mary, Life, and Wine

Immediately after Jesus entrusts the beloved disciple into the care of his mother and his mother in the care of the beloved disciple (John 19:26-27), we read that Jesus says: "After this, Jesus, knowing that all things had already been accomplished, in order that the Scripture would be fulfilled, said, "I am thirsty." The imagery of the cup of God's wrath is found in many places in the Hebrew Bible/Old Testament. One such place is found in Isaiah 51. There we read:

> 22 This is what your Sovereign LORD says, your God, who defends his people: "See, I have taken out of your hand the cup that made you stagger; from that cup, the goblet of my wrath, you will never drink again…" (Isa 51:22)

Now read again the above quoted words from the Gospel and allow the narrative to flow further to see the sequence of these enormously significant events. We read:

> 26 So when Jesus saw His mother, and the disciple whom He loved standing nearby, He said to His mother, "Woman, behold, your son!" 27 Then He said

to the disciple, "Behold, your mother!" And from that hour the disciple took her into his own household. [28] After this, Jesus, knowing that all things had already been accomplished, in order that the Scripture would be fulfilled, said, "I am thirsty." (John 19: 26-28)

This is very significant because it means that Jesus is now ready to drink of the cup of God's wrath. It is very important to realize that the timing for his request for a drink is not dictated by a physical need for a drink. No doubt, Jesus had already been thirsty for a long time, given the ordeal he underwent. We continue reading:

[29] A jar full of sour wine was standing there; so they put a sponge full of the sour wine on a branch of hyssop and brought it up to His mouth. [30] Therefore when Jesus had received the sour wine, He said, "It is finished!" And He bowed His head and gave up His spirit. (John 19: 29-30)

We will come back to the theme of wine later in this book. But now let us turn our attention back to the curious fact that both times we hear Jesus addressing his mother, he calls her "woman." Why? Even though the author of the Gospel of John does not tie the word "wine" to the idea of live-giving, another concept closely tied to Jesus' use of wine as a symbol – his blood. In John 6, the representatives and/or affiliates of the Judean authorities ("the Jews") are troubled by Jesus' claim that He is the bread of life that has come down from heaven (John 6:35-40). We read: "So then "the Jews" were complaining about Him because He said, "I am the bread that came down out of heaven." (John 6:41). As they continue to express their objections, Jesus makes several declarative arguments in return (John 6:42-51), although his arguments seem to have little effect:

[52] Then "the Jews" began to argue with one another, saying, "How can this man give us His flesh to eat?" [53] So Jesus said to them, "Truly, truly, I say to you, unless you eat the flesh of the Son of Man and

drink His blood, you have no life in yourselves. [54] The
one who eats My flesh and drinks My blood has
eternal life, and I will raise him up on the last
day. [55] For My flesh is true food, and My blood is tue
drink. [56] The one who eats My flesh and drinks My
blood remains in Me, and I in him. (John 6:52-56).

It is abundantly clear that Jesus believes – and the readers of
the Gospel of John are expected to believe it as well – that his
blood together with his body is the ultimate source of life. In one
way or another, feeding on Jesus means having a way to life itself.
We also see wine and more particularly the vineyard, as being
connected to Jesus' very person and mission when we read John
15:

[1] "I am the true vine… [5] I am the vine, you are the
branches; the one who remains in Me, and I in
him bears much fruit, for apart from Me you can do
nothing… [7] If you remain in Me, and My words remain
in you, ask whatever you wish, and it will be done for
you. [8] My Father is glorified by this, that you bear
much fruit, and so prove to be My disciples. [9] Just
as the Father has loved Me, I also have loved you;
remain in My love. (John 15:1, 5-9)

It is in Luke 22:20 that Jesus clearly connects the ideas of
wine/vine/blood all together ("This cup, which is poured out for
you, is the new covenant in My blood"). The Apostle Paul later
confirms this tradition almost verbatim in his letter to Corinthians
(1 Cor 11:25). Now that the relationship between the topics of
wine/vine/blood/life is established, it becomes important to also
connect the curious fact that both episodes in which Jesus calls his
mother "woman" involve wine.

The very first miracle of Jesus was one of turning water into
wine, as depicted in John 2. This event marked the inauguration of
his ministry. Later, at the end of his journey, he drank vinegar,
which is wine gone bad, while on the cross. This moment,
described in John 19, marked the literal completion of Jesus'
earthly ministry. Notably, both the beginning and the end of Jesus'

ministry are connected to wine. Furthermore, Mary plays a pivotal role in both these events as it becomes possible to think that John's Gospel portrays her as a second Hava/Zoe/Eve/Life-giver.

While it is crucial to understand that the focus on life-giving is not primarily on Mary but on her Son, as seen in John 6 and John 15, we cannot ignore Mary's role. She brought Him into the world, linking her directly to His life and work. And that is no small thing at all!

Early Church Fathers

It is important to ask the question of how early in Church history Christ-followers began to think about Mary as a second Eve. In other words, did this idea surface for the first time many centuries later, or was it already known in the first couple of centuries? Let us briefly review some of the voices that are still relevant today yet originated so long ago. One Christian apologist of the 2nd century was Justin Martyr, who wrote in the year 160 CE/AD:

> [Jesus] became man by the Virgin, in order that the disobedience which proceeded from the serpent might receive its destruction in the same way it derived its origin. For Eve, who was a virgin and undefiled, having conceived the word of the serpent, brought forth disobedience and death. But the Virgin Mary received faith and joy when the angel Gabriel announced the good tidings to her that the Spirit of the Lord would come upon her, and the power of the Highest would overshadow her: wherefore also the Holy Thing begotten of her is the Son of God; and she replied, 'Be it unto me according to your word.' (Dialogue with Trypho, 100)

Irenaeus of Lyon, a leading Christian priest and theologian also of the 2nd century, wrote in 180 CE/AD:

> It was that the knot of Eve's disobedience was loosed by the obedience of Mary. For what the virgin Eve had

bound fast through unbelief, this did the virgin Mary set free through faith. (Against Heresies, III.22.4)

For just as [Eve] was led astray by the word of an angel, so that she fled from God when she had transgressed His word; so, did [Mary], by an angelic communication, receive the glad tidings that she should sustain God, being obedient to His word. (Against Heresies, V.19.1)

Tertullian, another Christian theologian from the 2nd century, wrote:

… As Eve had believed the serpent, so Mary believed the angel. The delinquency which the one occasioned by believing, the other by believing effaced… But (it will be said) Eve did not at the devil's word conceive in her womb. Well, she at all events conceived; for the devil's word afterwards became as seed to her that she should conceive as an outcast and bring forth in sorrow. Indeed, she gave birth to a fratricidal devil; while Mary, on the contrary, bare one who was one day to secure salvation to Israel, His own brother after the flesh, and the murderer of Himself. (The Flesh of Christ, 17)

While many more fathers can be cited, one perhaps deserves special mention even though he lived even later. Augustine, one of the most significant Christian theologians and philosophers of the 4th century, writes:

Our Lord… was not averse to males, for he took the form of a male, nor to females, for of a female he was born. Besides, there is a great mystery here: that just as death comes to us through a woman, life is born to us through a woman; that the devil, defeated, would be tormented by each nature, feminine and masculine, as he had taken delight in the defection of both. (Christian Combat 22.24, 396 CE/AD)

I do not cite these early Christian Bible interpreters as some kind of "proof" that Mary is the second Eve, but simply as a testimony to show that this idea already exists shortly after the composition of the Gospels. This testimony of the Church Fathers certainly seems to say a lot more than the Gospels or the rest of the New Testament do about Mary, but my point is that it says it relatively early in Christian history. These ideas survive to our day in Catholic traditions from the times close to when Jesus and Mary walked the dusty roads of ancient Israel.

New Eve in Paul?

Apostle Paul writes that Jesus is born of a woman in one of his letters (Gal 4:4). But in that case, it seems to refer to the humanity of Jesus and not to the idea that Mary is a second Eve. In fact, quite the opposite seems to be the case with Paul. He appears completely unaware of this concept and does not seem to display it in any of his writings. For example, he writes:

> [20] But the fact is, Christ has been raised from the dead, the first fruits of those who are asleep. [21] For since by a man death came, by a man also came the resurrection of the dead. [22] For as in Adam all die, so also in Christ all will be made alive. [23] But each in his own order: Christ the first fruits, after that those who are Christ's at His coming... (1 Cor 15:20-23)

For example, consider Chapter 5 of Romans. There we read:

> [12] Therefore, just as through one man sin entered into the world, and death through sin, and so death spread to all mankind because all sinned... For if by the offense of the one the many died, much more did the grace of God and the gift by the grace of the one Man, Jesus Christ, overflow to the many... [19] For as through the one man's disobedience the many were made sinners, so also through the obedience of the One the many will be made righteous. (Rom 5:12-21)

71

It seems that Paul is rather insistent that Adam alone – not Adam and Eve as a couple – cast humanity into death by his actions. When Eve tastes the forbidden fruit, it seems that Paul understands humanity as still unfallen. From his writings, it seems that only when *Adam* tastes the forbidden fruit does humanity fall from the state of grace into the state of death.

But are we really justified in this conclusion based on the Apostle Paul neglecting to mention Eve in the iconic text above? Did Eve also not play a very significant, indeed a key role, in the fall of humanity? Can we really separate Adam from Eve, as Paul seems to do? In other words, when Paul writes that "in Adam all die", does he mean Adam alone or is it possible that he is simply following the literary canons of his time, saying "Adam" but meaning "Adam and Eve?"

This is where it would be advisable to recall our previous discussion about the Jewish concept of the Merits of the Fathers. If you recall, we concluded that even though the phraseology avoids any mention of Israel's mothers, they are, in fact, very much involved! The Jewish idea of "Merits of the Mothers" is included in the overall concept of the "Merits of the Fathers."[14]

Taking this argument into consideration is it then not possible that a similar dynamic is taking place here in Paul's writings as well?! We should explore this possibility of Paul following the verbal and conceptual canons of his time, mentioning Adam alone but, in fact, meaning Adam and Eve together. To do so, we need to ask ourselves two questions: Could that work, and is there any further evidence in Paul's words that may help to corroborate this point? We read in Paul's much-debated text from 1 Timothy 2:

> [8] Therefore, I want the men in every place to pray, lifting up holy hands, without anger and dispute. [9] Likewise, *I* want women to adorn themselves

---

[14] Gribetz, Sarit Kattan. "Zekhut Imahot: Mothers, Fathers, and Ancestral Merit in Rabbinic Sources." *Journal for the Study of Judaism in the Persian, Hellenistic, and Roman Period* 49, no. 2 (2018): 263–96. https://www.jstor.org/stable/26551249.

with proper clothing, modestly and discreetly, not with braided hair and gold or pearls or expensive apparel, [10] but rather by means of good works, as is proper for women making a claim to godliness. [11] A woman must quietly receive instruction with entire submissiveness. [12] But I do not allow a woman to teach or to exercise authority over a man, but to remain quiet. [13] For it was Adam who was first created, and then Eve. [14] And it was not Adam who was deceived, but the woman was deceived and became a wrongdoer. [15] But women will be preserved through childbirth—if they continue in faith, love, and sanctity, with moderation. (1 Tim 2:8-15)

Without getting into the many issues that arise from reading this text in our modern world (I invite you to read my other book, "The Jewish Apostle Paul: Rethinking One of the Greatest Jews That Ever Lived"), let us concentrate on vs. 13-14. Paul seems to argue that the reason a woman must not teach a man and that it should be the other way around is this: 1) God creates man first and Eve second, and 2) Eve is deceived and becomes a wrongdoer first.

Considering this, for the Apostle Paul, Eve seems to carry a lot of guilt in what happened back in Genesis. No doubt Paul knows this Torah story very well. Eve eats the fruit and then serves it to Adam. In so doing, she participates in Adam's offense. This adds strength to the argument that when Paul speaks of Adam, he speaks of the story, events, and personalities (Adam and Eve together), and not about the figure of Adam alone.

In other words, does Paul include in Adam the figure of Eve just the way the Merits of the Fathers in later rabbinic thought includes the Merits of the mothers? Perhaps.

Is There Really Mary in Revelation?

As I came to Revelation 12's description of a heavenly queen about to give birth to the one who will rule the nations with an iron rod (obviously Jesus). I could not help but to ask myself an unexpected question: Could the heavenly queen be Mary? We read:

> A woman clothed with the sun, and the moon under her feet, and on her head a crown of twelve stars; and she was pregnant, and she cried out, being in labor and in pain to give birth. (Rev 12:1-2)[15]

The identity of the woman is not completely clear, but what is beyond doubt is that, in some way, the woman is the mother of Jesus because later, we read: "She gave birth to a son, a male, who is going to rule all the nations with a rod of iron." (Rev 12:5) The concept of ruling with an iron rod comes directly from Psalm 2. There we read:

> [7] I will announce the decree of the LORD: He said to Me, 'You are My Son, Today I have fathered You. [8] Ask *it* of Me, and I will certainly give the nations as Your inheritance, And the ends of the earth as Your possession. [9] You shall break them with a rod of iron,

---

[15] The immediate problem most Catholics encounter upon reading this text (Rev 12:1-2) has to do with the Catholic belief that Mary (due to her exemption from the wages of sin) did not suffer pain during the birth of Jesus. Many Catholic theologians sought to explain this reference, with various levels of success, clearly indicating that, indeed, the woman had a fully human experience like all other mothers – pain at birth. This is when it is good to know that I am not a Catholic but simply exploring ideas that Catholics have about our shared Scripture.

You shall shatter them like earthenware.' (Psalm 2:7-9)

The Apostle Paul's preaching in Antioch links Psalm 2 to Christ:

> [32] And we preach to you the good news of the promise made to the fathers, [33] that God has fulfilled this promise to those of us who are the descendants by raising Jesus, as it is also written in the second Psalm: 'YOU ARE MY SON; TODAY I HAVE FATHERED YOU.' (Acts 13:32-33)

Christ at his future second coming is described similarly. We read:

> [11] And I saw heaven opened, and behold, a white horse, and He who sat on it is called Faithful and True, and in righteousness, He judges and wages war... [15] From His mouth comes a sharp sword, so that with it He may strike down the nations, and He will rule them with a rod of iron... (Rev 19:11-15)[16]

Knowing what John believes about Jesus' messiahship, we can be quite certain that Revelation chapter 12 depicts King Jesus as the child born of the heavenly woman. This leaves us with three main interpretive options. First, the woman is Mary, the literal earthly mother of Jesus. Second, the woman is either Israel or the Church, whose anointed Son will rule the world. The third option is that the woman is a hybrid image of Mary and Israel and/or Church.

---

[16] It is intriguing that not only Christ, but Christ-followers as well can expect to join Christ's rule over the nations characterized by the presence of the iron rod: "The one who overcomes, and the one who keeps My deeds until the end, I will give him authority over the nations; AND HE SHALL RULE THEM WITH A ROD OF IRON...". (Rev 2:26-27)

Woman as Mary

Let us briefly recall our exploration of Luke's birth narrative, where we see the high honor given to Mary.

> Now in the sixth month the angel Gabriel was sent from God to a city in Galilee named Nazareth, to a virgin betrothed to a man whose name was Joseph, of the descendants of David; and the virgin's name was Mary. And coming in, he said to her, "Greetings, favored one! The Lord is with you." (Lk 1:26-28)

In Luke's Gospel, Mary finds great favor in God's sight by gaining the unique and awesome privilege of becoming the mother of Jesus Christ. Since we know Jesus is the one who will rule the nations with an iron rod, could it be that Mary is the one depicted as the "woman clothed with the sun" in Revelation 12? Possibly.

What may strengthen this case is that other designations in Revelation also refer to a specific individual. For example, "dragon" refers to Satan, and the Son "that will rule with an iron rod" to Jesus. I conclude that if the woman described as being clothed with the sun does not also refer to an individual, which is still possible, it would seem somewhat out of character for this vision.

Woman as Israel/Church

Now, let us briefly consider whether the woman depicted in Rev 12:5 can be understood not as a singular person but as the image of Israel, God's chosen people. We read in Deuteronomy:

> I will raise up for them a prophet from among their countrymen like you, and I will put My words in his mouth, and he shall speak to them everything that I command him. (Deut 18:18)

So it is that the Messiah, as later Jewish and Christian traditions understand in Deuteronomy 18:18, will come from Israel. In other words, Israel, in some way, can be seen as the people group giving birth/mothering this future Messianic figure. In his letter to the Romans, Paul traces the messianic promises through Israel as well:

> [1] I am telling the truth in Christ, I am not lying; my conscience testifies with me in the Holy Spirit, [2] that I have great sorrow and unceasing grief in my heart. [3] For I could wish that I myself were accursed, separated from Christ for the sake of my countrymen, my kinsmen according to the flesh, [4] who are Israelites, to whom belongs the adoption as sons and daughters, the glory, the covenants, the giving of the Law, the temple service, and the promises; [5] whose are the fathers, and from whom is the Messiah according to the flesh, who is over all, God blessed forever. Amen. (Rom 9:1-5)

There is another example that is extremely important for understanding what or who the mother of the Messiah can be or can symbolize. In Galatians, Paul writes, "But the Jerusalem above is free; she is our mother." (Gal 4:26). The heavenly Jerusalem is allegorically connected to God's people, Israel.

The above texts are excellent examples that can justify the view that the people of Israel corporately could be allegorically understood as "the mother" of the Messiah Jesus. Revelation 11-13, however, contain five references to various periods of time that may help us to determine the identity of the woman in this vision:

> Leave out the courtyard which is outside the temple and do not measure it, because it has been given to the nations; and they will trample the holy city for forty-two months. (Rev 11:2)

> And I will grant authority to my two witnesses, and they will prophesy for 1,260 days, clothed in sackcloth. (Rev 11:3)

> Then the woman fled into the wilderness where she had a place prepared by God, so that there she would be nourished for 1,260 days. (Rev 12:6)

But the two wings of the great eagle were given to the
woman, so that she could fly into the wilderness to her
place, where she was nourished for a time, times, and
half a time, away from the presence of the serpent.
(Rev 12:14)

A mouth was given to him, speaking arrogant words
and blasphemies, and authority to act for forty-two
months was given to him. (Rev 13:5)

First, according to solar rendering, there are 30 days in a
month. How many days are there in 42 months? The answer is
1,260 days. Second, 42 months is how many years? Since there are
12 months in a year, 42 months equal to 3 ½ years, which is
probably the equivalent of "a time (1 year), and times (2 years),
and half a time (half a year)" as used in12:14. The math is $1 + 2 + ½ = 3 ½$. So far, everything lines up.

These calculations, summaries, and references bring us to the
conclusion that all three periods of time are the same: 1260 days =
42 months = 3 ½ years. This probably means that the various
pictures/visions/images that Revelation presents are really referring
to one and the same thing – God's people undergoing persecution
and eventually coming out victorious.

Woman as Israel and Mary

Is it possible to say that this is a hybrid image? In the first
broader way, the woman refers to Israel - Messiah's own people,
but in a narrower way, it refers to Mary, the particular Israelite
woman who bore Jesus. Which one is true? I will show that the
answer may be both. If the woman is not merely Israel but is also
Mary, then we must explain the following:

Then the woman fled into the wilderness, where she
had a place prepared by God so that there, she would
be nourished for 1,260 days. (Rev 12:6)

A possible way to understand this is the story found in the Gospel of Mathew. In this scenario, Herod seeking to destroy the newborn Jesus – and all Jewish boys just to be sure – would be understood as the Dragon's representative, who stood to devour the child (Rev 12:4). As we read in Matthew 2:7-15:

> [7] Then Herod secretly called for the magi and determined from them the exact time the star appeared. [8] And he sent them to Bethlehem and said, "Go and search carefully for the child; and when you have found Him, report to me, so that I too may come and worship Him." …[12] And after being warned by God in a dream not to return to Herod, the magi left for their own country by another way. [13] Now when they had gone, behold, an angel of the Lord appeared to Joseph in a dream and said, "Get up! Take the child and His mother and flee to Egypt, and stay there until I tell you; for Herod is going to search for the child to kill Him." [14] So Joseph got up and took the child and His mother while it was still night, and left for Egypt. [15] He stayed there until the death of Herod… (Matt 2:7-15)

We continue reading in Matt 2:16-20 that:

> [16] Then when Herod saw that he had been tricked by the magi, he became very enraged, and sent men and killed all the boys who were in Bethlehem and all its vicinity who were two years old or under, according to the time which he had determined from the magi. (Matt 2:16-20)

One can suppose that 1,260 days might be somehow connected to the period when Mary, Joseph, and Jesus were hiding in Egypt. The story in Matthew does not give us that exact time, so it is impossible to say if the 1,260 days refer to this story or not. If it does, it probably does not do so literally. The woman in Revelation is also described as having a crown of 12 stars. There are also three possibilities here: Twelve stars can represent 12 tribes of Israel or the 12 apostles of Israel, or some combination of the two. Basically, these descriptions seem to support our third option, where the woman that gives birth to the Messiah is a hybrid image of Israel as God's ancient people and Mary, Mother of King Jesus, as a physical Jewish mother. We read:

> Then another sign appeared in heaven: and behold, a great red dragon having seven heads and ten horns, and on his heads were seven crowns. And his tail swept away a third of the stars of heaven and hurled them to the earth. And the dragon stood before the woman who was about to give birth, so that when she gave birth, he might devour her child. (Rev 12:3-4)

A mythical, seven-headed, red dragon appears in the skies. He is crowned and is very powerful, and the seven horns are symbols of the fullness of power. The bloodthirsty dragon positions himself in such a way that it would be possible for him to destroy the male child that the woman is about to birth. He is standing ready to devour the child even prior to his birth, anticipating his murderous meal. Probably one of the most important texts underlying the Catholic idea of calling Mary "Mary, Mother of Jesus" is found in Revelation 12:17. There we read:

> So the dragon was enraged with the woman and went off to make war with the rest of her children, who keep the commandments of God and hold to the testimony of Jesus. (Rev 12:17)

The narrative within the Book of Revelation doesn't simply convey that the Dragon, or Satan, is outrightly defeated. Like any conflict, there are repercussions following defeat. Satan, banished to earth, aimed to obliterate the life of Jesus, both during his birth and at the time of the crucifixion. However, his evil intentions fail, as depicted in Revelation 12:13-16. Unable to claim victory, the Dragon seeks to wreak as much havoc as possible, turning his destructive attention towards the other children of the woman. We read that the dragon: "…went off to make war with the rest of her children." (Rev 12:17). No matter what the identity of the Woman is (Mary, Israel/Church, or both), the rest of the woman's children clearly refers to all the believers in Israel's God in Christ.

In summary, let me say that the available data does not allow me to be dogmatic about the identity of the "woman clothed with the sun." However, if either the physical Virgin Mary or the hybrid interpretation of Mary/Israel/Church is correct, then the Protestant portrayal of Catholics elevating Mary too high up in their spiritual life, becomes a moot point indeed. At the very least, Protestant Christians should stop demonizing Catholics in their minds but rather think of them as brothers and sisters with whose interpretation of the Scriptures they disagree. This, in and of itself, would be a wonderful result of our so far inconclusive study.

Is Mary Really a New Queen Mother?

Throughout Church history, Mary of Nazareth has received several different names and titles from a wide variety of Catholic and Orthodox believers around the world. Among some of the most recognized are Mary, Mother of Jesus, Blessed Virgin Mary, Mary Mother of God, and of course, Queen of Heaven. In the previous chapter, we discussed one of the reasons that many Christians worldwide consider Mary to be far more than just another biblical character. We have looked at how it is possible to view Revelation 12 as a hybrid image of Israel/Church and Mary of Nazareth.

In this section, I would like to examine another claim that Catholic theologians make about the Queenship of Mary. The argument is based on the collection of Old Testament/Hebrew Bible scriptures that seem to report that mothers of Judean kings (there is a big question about Kings of Israel) had special status and, indeed, an active role in the courts of their sons. They are not simply women who happen to be the mothers of kings, but they have a special position that, by various accounts, encompasses many different aspects that set them apart from everyone else in the kingdom. In other words, in each royal court, there was a King and a Queen, who was not his wife but rather his mother.

The Catholic argument is clear: if Jesus is a Judaic King, his mother holds a unique status. This status is second only to her Son's status in God's kingdom, reflecting the tradition of the mothers of previous Judaic kings.

The Mothers of Judean Kings

The first part of this argument emphasizes that 1 and 2 Kings carefully preserve the names of an overwhelming majority of the mothers of Judean kings (1 Kgs 14:21; 15:1-2, 9-10; 22:41-42; 2 Kgs 8:25-26; 12:1; 14:1-2; 15:1-2, 32-33; 21:1; 21:19; 22:1; 23:31, 36; 24:8; 24:18). Only two mothers, those of Jehoram and Ahaz, are left out (2 Kgs 8:16; 2 Kgs 16:1). For example, we read that:

> [21] Now Rehoboam the son of Solomon reigned in Judah. Rehoboam was forty-one years old when he became king, and he reigned for seventeen years in Jerusalem, the city which the LORD had chosen from all the tribes of Israel to put His name there. And his mother's name was Naamah of the Ammonites. (1 Kgs 14:21)

Also, we read:

> [1] Now in the eighteenth year of King Jeroboam, the son of Nebat, Abijam became king over Judah. [2] He reigned for three years in Jerusalem; and his mother's name was Maacah the daughter of Abishalom. (1 Kgs 15:1-2)

And that:

> [25] In the twelfth year of Joram the son of Ahab king of Israel, Ahaziah the son of Jehoram king of Judah began to reign. [26] Ahaziah was twenty-two years old when he became king, and he reigned for one year in Jerusalem. And his mother's name was Athaliah the granddaughter of Omri king of Israel. (2 Kgs 8:25-26)

It is very clear from the above three selections that a king's mother is important enough to be mentioned in the Bible by name in most cases. The question is, what best explains why this is so? One possible answer is that they have a particular role to play in the kingdoms of their sons. In other words, they are mothers to kings, but there is a lot more to it than that. They have a powerful status that is second only in status to that of their own royal sons.

What is Gebira?

The second part of the argument is based on the idea *gebira* (in Hebrew, this means something like "powerful woman/strong woman/courageous woman) is an official title in the royal courts of Judea and that Mary, in her motherhood of Jesus must be understood in this context. She is the ultimate *Gebira*, our Catholic brothers and sisters would argue because her son Jesus is the ultimate Judean King. Is it possible that they are right? Let us investigate this topic with an open mind but a discerning spirit.

The noun *gebira* or *geberet* occurs 15 times in the Hebrew Bible with the general meaning of "lady", "great lady", "mistress", or even a "queen" (Gen 16:4, 8-9; 1 Kgs 15:13; 2 Kgs 5:3; 10:13; Isa 24:2; 47:5, 7; Jer 13:18; 29:2; Ps 123:2; Prov 30:23; 2 Chr 15:16). Nineteen queen mothers are specifically mentioned. One hails from the era of the unified monarchy, Bathsheba. Another is a northerner whose reign appears more "southern" in its essence, Jezebel, who is called *gebira* by southern visitors. The rest, a group of seventeen, are identified as *gebira*, originating from Judah during the time of the divided monarchy.[17] Now, the meaning of the word is not conclusive, and various scholars sharply disagree with one another due to the lack of sufficient evidence. For example, Niels-Erik Andreasen, a seven-day Adventist scholar, writes:

> …it soon becomes obvious from the text that the queen mother was not merely treated with deference by the monarch, but that she held a significant official political position superseded only by that of the king himself. The evidence for this is near at hand. Bathsheba enjoyed access to and held influence over Solomon (1 Kgs 2:13- 25), and she played an

---

[17] Ackerman, Susan. "The Queen Mother and the Cult in Ancient Israel." *Journal of Biblical Literature* 112, no. 3 (1993): 385–401. https://doi.org/10.2307/3267740.

important role in securing his accession (1 Kgs 1:11-31). Maacah displayed an active and apparently unorthodox interest in the cult, whereupon king Asa took the unusual step of dismissing her (1 Kgs 15:13). Jezebel, the only known queen mother in Israel, was taken as seriously as the king by visiting dignitaries from Judah (2 Kgs 10:13). Athaliah was able to usurp entirely the throne in Jerusalem and to hold it for some six years (2 Kgs 11). Nehushta, the queen mother, and king Jehoiachin shared a ceremonial moment on thrones, wearing crowns (Jer 13:18).[18]

As recorded in 2 Samuel 11:3, Bathsheba, Eliam's daughter, is recognized as the inaugural Queen Mother. Her figure sets the groundwork for the esteemed role of the queen mother. Bathsheba's request to her son Solomon on Adonijah's behalf (1 Kgs 2:13-25) implies that the queen mother's status is on par with that of the monarch. The king's deference to Bathsheba — he greets her standing, bows to her, and places her on his right — emphasizes her elevated position. Her story suggests that the Queen Mother is the primary counselor to the king, representing the populace and the court.

Another significant example of the queen mother's high standing is Maacah, Abishalom's daughter (1 Kgs 15:2). As per 1 Kgs 15:13, Asa ousts his mother, Maacah, from her role of queen mother due to her construction of a detestable Asherah image. This incident lays the groundwork for the idea that the Queen Mother wields substantial power, especially in religious matters. Further evidence of the queen mother's remarkable influence and power comes from Hamutal, Jeremiah of Libnah's daughter (2 Kgs 23:31). Famous for being the mother of two kings, Jehoahaz and Zedekiah, she serves as a potent testament to the queen mother's influence.

Nehushta, Elnathan's daughter (2 Kgs 24:8), is too an example tied to the Queen Mother's office. Her mention right after

---

[18] Andreasen, Niels-Erik A. "The Role of the Queen Mother in Israelite Society." *The Catholic Biblical Quarterly* 45, no. 2 (1983): 179–94. http://www.jstor.org/stable/43719002.

her son, King Jehoiachin, in the account of those exiled to Babylon (2 Kgs 24:15), signals her importance and high status. Another case that supports this theory is that of Jezebel, daughter of Ethbaal, the Sidonian king and wife to King Ahab (1 Kgs 16:31). Her sons' visit to the royal princes and the queen mother's sons suggests her high position (2 Kgs 10:13).

Lastly, Athaliah, either Ahab's daughter (2 Kgs 8:18) or Omri's daughter (2 Kgs 8:26), is credited for her takeover of the kingdom following the royal family's demise. Her capability to commandeer the kingdom emphasizes the significant power that comes with the role of queen mother.[19] On the other hand, Israeli scholar Zafira Ben-Barak argues that the case for *gebira* having a particular role in Judean courts is extremely weak, and ultimately unjustified. She expresses frustrations with other scholars' conclusions:

> …it's important to note that the *Gebirah*, or Queen Mother, was a significant figure in the royal courts of Judah and Israel. However, only in the cases of four Queen Mothers - Bathsheba, Maacah, Hamutal, and Nehushta - do the historical texts delve into any detail about these individuals. Each of these women was associated with the House of David. Given the limited and sporadic instances, it's puzzling why scholars have drawn conclusions about the *Gebirah* based on such a small sample size. Rather than considering them as isolated exceptions, these few cases have led to broad assertions about the *Gebirah*'s role and influence.
> …Therefore, it's premature to formulate a general rule or comprehensive theory about the *Gebirah*'s role as a state office based on such limited and meager evidence compared to the total number of known queen mothers.[20]

As you can see from the samples of quotations above, the

---

[19] Ben-Barak, Zafrira. "The Status and Right of the Gĕbîrâ." *Journal of Biblical Literature* 110, no. 1 (1991): 23–34. https://doi.org/10.2307/3267147.
[20] Ben-Barak, Zafrira. "The Status and Right of the Gĕbîrâ." *Journal of Biblical Literature* 110, no. 1 (1991): 23–34. https://doi.org/10.2307/3267147.

evidence can indeed be taken either way. There is a good case to be made for the Queenship of Mary based on the possible special status of the mothers of the Judean kings. It is certainly a plausible and interesting argument. But again, the case is not ironclad. The evidence is read as sufficient by some and unconvincing by others.

I acknowledge that this chapter probably felt a lot heavier to you in comparison to the preceding ones, both because of scholarly quotations and because of the abundance of Old Testament references that most modern believers are simply not familiar with. I trust you will forgive me for the more difficult contents of this chapter and are still willing to accompany me on the rest of this journey. Besides, aren't you curious about what comes next?

REQUEST

Dear reader, may I ask you for a favor? If you are enjoying this book, would you take three minutes of your time and provide encouraging feedback to other people about this book? Look up "The Jewish Roots of Mary" **on Amazon.com and write a brief review! After that, please drop me a personal note and let me know that you did so - dr.eli.israel@gmail.com. Thank you so much for your support and encouragement!**

In His Grace,

Dr. Eli Lizorkin-Eyzenberg

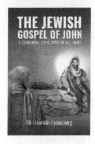

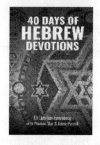
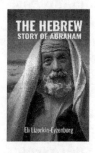

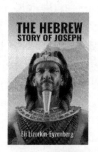

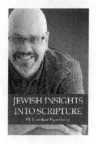

Is Mary Really a New Ark?

The last key argument that Catholics commonly make to substantiate their views on Mary is that, in their opinion, the Gospel of Luke, though not solely, makes an intentional connection between the Old Testament ark of the covenant and Mary of Nazareth as its new Covenant manifestation. For a Protestant, largely unfamiliar with any such connections, this may be a surprising claim. Let us now turn our attention to examine if this Catholic argument has merit.

We should begin at the beginning. The Ark of the Covenant is one of the most fascinating topics for Christians. As mentioned before, it was housed in the Holy of Holies in the Tabernacle that traveled with the Israelites throughout their journey and later comes to reside in the Jerusalem Temple. While not all Biblical stories connected with the ark of the covenant feature it within this sacred space, its most common "docking station" was indeed the Holy of Holies. Once each year the high priest of Israel would enter the Holy of Holies, sprinkling the blood of sacrifice upon the mercy seat (the cover of the ark) to obtain forgiveness of sins for the entire nation of Israel. We read:

> [10] Now they shall construct an ark of acacia wood two and a half cubits long, one and a half cubits wide, and one and a half cubits high. [11] You shall overlay it with pure gold, inside and out you shall overlay it, and you shall make a gold molding around it. (Ex 25:10-11)

Acacia wood is one of the most, if not *the* most, durable wood on the planet. The container is to house three sacred objects

– more about this soon – and to be laid with gold, the symbol of royalty, holiness, and purity, from within and from without. No human hand is to touch it. For this reason, special golden rings are made so that the priests, using poles, which are also made of acacia wood and overlaid with gold, can carry the ark as needed. We read:

> [12] You shall also cast four gold rings for it and fasten them on its four feet; two rings shall be on one side of it, and two rings on the other side of it. [13] And you shall make poles of acacia wood and overlay them with gold. [14] You shall put the poles into the rings on the sides of the ark, to carry the ark with them. [15] The poles shall remain in the rings of the ark; they shall not be removed from it. [16] You shall put into the ark the testimony which I shall give you. (Ex 25:12-15)

The ark's significance is derived from God's order to have his testimony placed inside. The utter holiness of this container is based on the presence of this testimony. God continues to instruct Moses about how the ark should look. We read:

> [17] And you shall make an atoning cover of pure gold, two and a half cubits long and one and a half cubits wide. [18] You shall make two cherubim of gold; make them of hammered work at the two ends of the atoning cover. [19] Make one cherub at one end and one cherub at the other end; you shall make the cherubim of one piece with the atoning cover at its two ends. [20] And the cherubim shall have their wings spread upward, covering the atoning cover with their wings and facing one another; the faces of the cherubim are to be turned toward the atoning cover. [21] Then you shall put the atoning cover on top of the ark, and in the ark you shall put the testimony which I will give to you. (Ex 25:17-21)

The description is very precise. The size of the lid must match the holy container itself. Two statues made of gold must be in the form of cherubim. Their wings must be spread upward as they face one another, covering the sacred lid – the atoning cover. The significance of this sacred lid cannot possibly be understated for it is from there YHVH promises to speak to Moses. We read:

> ²² There I will meet with you; and from above the atoning cover, from between the two cherubim which are upon the ark of the testimony, I will speak to you about every commandment that I will give you for the sons of Israel. (Ex 25:22)

What made the ark of the covenant to serve as the epicenter of God's presence in the sacred Israelite space? Simple. Its inner contents and its very special lid. All its inner contents have to do with God's holy deeds in the early history of Israel. Three sacred items are hidden inside: 1) the tablets with the Ten Commandments, 2) manna from heaven, and 3) the budded rod of Aaron. (At the end of this chapter you will find a surprising turn to my own discovery regarding this. Please resist the temptation to fast-forward now, but I decided to leave my earlier argument as it is so that I can turn it into a wonderful teaching opportunity.) All three are powerful symbolic reminders of God's actions.

First, the Ten Commandments symbolize all of God's word that will be given to Israel to guide the basic societal order into the future. Second, manna symbolizes God's provision of life's sustenance to the children of Israel during their travel in the wilderness. And third, the budded rod of Aaron is a reminder to the rebellious about God's full and unconditional endorsement of the Levitical priesthood, "Return Aaron's staff before the ark of the covenant law, to be preserved as a token for the rebellious." (Num 17:10). The basic idea here is that YHVH manifests himself to Israel through his acts of lordship (the Ten Commandments), provision (manna from heaven) and the acts of mediation/priesthood (Aaron's rod).

The Epicenter of God's Presence

On the one hand, it is understood that YHVH is present everywhere. On the other hand, what we read in Isaiah is also true. We read: "This is what the LORD says: "Heaven is My throne and the earth is the footstool for My feet. Where then is a house you could build for Me? And where is a place that I may rest?" (Isa 66:1)

God does not need a physical place on earth to call home. The prophet Isaiah also tells us that in some sense God dwells not only in his heavenly Temple but also among the meek and lowly on earth. We read:

> For this is what the high and exalted One who lives forever, whose name is Holy, says: "I dwell in a high and holy place, and also with the contrite and lowly of spirit in order to revive the spirit of the lowly and to revive the heart of the contrite. (Isa 57:15)

Even though all the above is right and true, there is a sense in which YHVH's presence had gradations. For example, while God dwells on earth and is everywhere present, He particularly dwells among His people in the Promised Land. While He dwells with his people in the Promised Land, he dwells in a special way in the Holy City of Jerusalem. While He dwells in Jerusalem, he dwells in a unique way in Zion, God's holy mountain. While He dwells in God's Zion, He dwells even more, especially in His Temple. While He dwells in His Temple, he particularly dwells in the Holy of Holies. While He dwells in the Holy of Holies, the very epicenter of His dwelling is in the ark of the covenant. The higher the concentration of God's presence, the greater the level of holiness is ascribed to those sacred places. The greater the level of holiness and God's presence, the less He encounters the human agent due to the perfection of YHVH and the imperfection of His fallen creation.

Ark Outside of the Holy of Holies

However, some of the most powerful stories where the Ark of the Covenant is featured have to do with events outside of the Holy of Holies. Several key stories are truly worth recalling because they offer further clarity about the meaning and function of the sacred ark. In the third chapter of Joshua, we learn of the

Israelites' need to traverse the Jordan River to reach the Promised Land. Directions are issued to follow the priests who bear the ark of the covenant. The priests carry the ark into the river, and the waters are halted to allow the Israelites to cross. Once all have reached the other side, the ark is removed, and the waters once again fill the river (Josh 3). The presence of God in and/or through the ark affects this deliverance.

As the Israelites progress on their journey and find themselves confronted by Jericho's wall, the ark once again plays a pivotal role. Joshua is commanded by the Lord to have armed men march around the wall for six days. The procession includes priests blowing trumpets, followed by the ark of the covenant. On the seventh day, the marching army is instructed to shout loudly, and the walls of Jericho fall. The presence and power of God are manifested in the ark-led army and lead to the fall of Jericho's walls (Josh 6).

The significance of the ark is reaffirmed in 1 Samuel. The Israelites are engaged in battle with the Philistines, losing badly. They decide to retrieve the ark, hoping its presence would assist them in defeating their foes. The arrival of the ark causes the Philistines to fear that a deity has entered the camp. They fight and defeat the Israelites, capturing the sacred artifact. The Philistines place their trophy in Dagon's temple, but their god's statue keeps falling before the ark. The Lord brings more destruction upon the Philistines, leading them to rid themselves of the stolen Israelite sacred object by relocating it to the city of Gath. However, Gath experiences the same severe hardships, and consequently, the ark is transferred to a third city, where disaster again strikes. After seven months, the Philistines decide to return the ark to the Israelites (1 Samuel 4-5).

The Philistines return the stolen ark, accompanied by golden guilt offerings on a cart (1 Sam 6). The cows attached to the cart direct it towards Beth Shemesh, and the people celebrate its return. The cart halts in Joshua's field near a large stone. The Levites take the ark and place it on the stone, offering sacrifices and burnt offerings to the Lord. However, because they look directly at God's presence, 70 people are killed. Uncertain of what to do next, they send a message to Kiriath Jearim, asking its inhabitants to retrieve the ark. The people of Kiriath Jearim come for the ark, bringing it to the house of Abinadab. His son safeguards the ark, which remains in the city for 20 years (1 Samuel 7).

David and the Ark

Relatively soon after David becomes Israel's king, we read the story in 2 Sam 6 of the ark of the covenant traveling from the house of Abinadab to Jerusalem. Here we find a very interesting description of the ark:

וַיָּקָם וַיֵּלֶךְ דָּוִד, וְכָל-הָעָם אֲשֶׁר אִתּוֹ, מִבַּעֲלֵי, יְהוּדָה-לְהַעֲלוֹת מִשָּׁם,
אֵת אֲרוֹן הָאֱלֹהִים, אֲשֶׁר-נִקְרָא שֵׁם שֵׁם יְהוָה צְבָאוֹת יֹשֵׁב הַכְּרֻבִים,
עָלָיו

[2] And David departed from Baale-Judah, with all the people who were with him, to bring up from there the ark of God which is called by the Name, the very name of the LORD of armies who is enthroned above the cherubim. (2 Sam 6:2)

A special new cart is brought in to carry the ark of the covenant. The house of Abinadab is situated on a hill. Two sons of Abinadab, Uzzah, and Ahio, are in charge (2 Sam 6:3). Ahio apparently is leading the way. While this was happening:

David and all the house of Israel were celebrating before the LORD with all kinds of instruments made of juniper wood, and with lyres, harps, tambourines, castanets, and cymbals. (2 Sam 6:5b)

Everything was going according to plan, and nothing could predict the tragic event that was about to take place. When Ahio and Uzzah reach the threshing floor of Nacon, the cart suddenly begins to tilt. It is all but certain that the sacred ark of the covenant would fall on the floor because the oxen nearly overturned it (2 Sam 6:6). While Uzzah was no doubt warned by his father never to touch the ark of the covenant with his bare hands, he instinctively reaches out his hand to steady the sacred object and prevent it from falling. Even though it is hard for us to understand God's action here, we read:

> [7] And the anger of the LORD burned against Uzzah, and God struck him down there for his irreverence; and he died there by the ark of God. (2 Sam 6:7).

ז וַיִּחַר-אַף יְהוָה בְּעֻזָּה, וַיַּכֵּהוּ שָׁם הָאֱלֹהִים עַל-הַשַּׁל; וַיָּמָת שָׁם, עִם אֲרוֹן הָאֱלֹהִים

The holiness of this object was so incredibly great that even Uzzah, who meant no disrespect and did not even have time to think before he reacted, is judged so severely. It is a tragedy indeed. David is angry. We read:

> [8] Then David became angry because of the LORD'S outburst against Uzzah; and that place has been called Perez-Uzzah to this day. [9] So David was afraid of the LORD that day; and he said, "How can the ark of the LORD come to me?" [10] And David was unwilling to move the ark of the LORD into the city of David with him; but David took it aside to the house of Obed-Edom, the Gittite. [11] The ark of the LORD remained in the house of Obed-Edom the Gittite for three months, and the LORD blessed Obed-Edom and all his household. (2 Sam 6:8-11)

One can almost imagine what went on in David's mind after this tragic event. He remembers full well what happened to the Philistines in three separate locations when they captured the ark. After the death of Uzzah, he probably anticipated a sequence of similar events, but these never came to be. Quite the opposite, actually. We read:

> [12] Now it was reported to King David, saying, "The LORD has blessed the house of Obed-Edom and all that belongs to him, on account of the ark of God." So David went and brought the ark of God up from the house of Obed-Edom to the city of David with joy…

[14] And David was dancing before the LORD with all his strength, and David was wearing a linen ephod. [15] So David and all the house of Israel were bringing up the ark of the LORD with joyful shouting and the sound of the trumpet. (2 Sam 6:12-15)

In Israel's history, the ark of the covenant is rightly considered both a very powerful tool to ensure Israel's survival through forgiveness and victory, and at the same time a very dangerous object that is to be treated with supreme holiness or suffer unanticipated consequences.

Mary and the Ark of the Covenant

Catholic theologians make an interesting claim to substantiate their belief that Mary is a New Testament ark of the covenant. This assertion is indeed very old, going back to many fathers of the Church. Here are two examples of the connection that many Church Fathers held. St. Hippolytus (c. 170-c. 236) wrote:

> "At that time, the Savior coming from the Virgin, the ark, brought forth His own Body into the world from that ark, which was gilded with pure gold within by the Word, and without by the Holy Ghost; so that the truth was shown forth, and the ark was manifested... And the Savior came into the world bearing the incorruptible ark, that is to say His own body" (S. Hippolytus, In Dan.vi., Patr. Gr., Tom. 10, p. 648).

Athanasius of Alexandria (c. 296–373) wrote:

> "O noble Virgin, truly you are greater than any other greatness. For who is your equal in greatness, O dwelling place of God the Word? To whom among all creatures shall I compare you, O Virgin? You are greater than them all O [Ark of the] Covenant, clothed with purity instead of gold! You are the ark in which is found the golden vessel containing the true manna, that

is, the flesh in which divinity resides" (Homily of the Papyrus of Turin).

Catholic theologians observe that the cloud of the Lord's glory covered or overshadowed the ark upon its completion. Vatican's Pontifical Council for the Pastoral Care of Migrants and Itinerant People has stated:

> "The Virgin Mary is the living shrine of the Word of God, the ark of the New and Eternal Covenant. In fact, Saint Luke's account of the Annunciation of the angel to Mary nicely incorporates the images of the tent of meeting with God in Sinai and of the Temple of Zion. Just as the cloud covered the people of God marching in the desert (cf. *Nm* 10:34; *Dt* 33:12; *Ps* 91:4) and just as the same cloud, as a sign of the divine mystery present in the midst of Israel, hovered over the ark of the covenant (cf. *Ex* 40:35), so now the shadow of the Most High envelops and penetrates the tabernacle of the new covenant that is the womb of Mary (cf. *Lk* 1:35)" (Vatican Council *The Shrine*, § 18).

This stands in line with other connections between the Old and New Testaments as Catholic believers have come to understand them. Another example of such a claimed parallel is that Mary, Mother of Jesus, is a New Testament fulfillment of Jacob's Ladder. But let us deal with the ark of the covenant first, since we will soon see how in Catholic interpretation of Revelation chapter 11 (with the appearance of the ark in the Heavenly Temple) and chapter 12 (with the woman clothed with the sun), will be tied into one theological construct.

Possible Parallels

In his book referred to several times from the beginning of my study, Brant Pitre writes that "...several striking parallels emerge..." between 2 Sam 6 and Luke 1 as well as between Luke and other ark-related texts.[21] I will first allow Brant Pitre to make his point and then I will follow with my own brief examination. Let me state at the outset that sometimes I will agree and find his arguments convincing and sometimes I will argue against it, showing why I remain open, but unconvinced.

Overshadowing of Mary

Brant Pitre raises several key points as to why he believes that Mary should be viewed as the New Testament fulfillment of the Old Testament ark of the covenant. This is a classic Catholic argument. In Exodus we read:

> [34] Then the cloud covered (וַיְכַס הֶעָנָן) the tent of meeting, and the glory of the LORD (וּכְבוֹד יְהוָה) filled the tabernacle. [35] And Moses was not able to enter the tent of meeting because the cloud had settled on it (כִּי-שָׁכַן עָלָיו הֶעָנָן), and the glory of the LORD filled the tabernacle (וּכְבוֹד יְהוָה, מָלֵא אֶת-הַמִּשְׁכָּן). (Exodus 40:34-35)

In the Gospel of Luke we read:

> [35] The angel answered and said to her, "The Holy Spirit will come upon you (ἐπελεύσεται ἐπὶ σέ), and the power of the Most High will overshadow (ἐπισκιάσει) you; for that reason also the holy Child will be called the Son of God. (Luke 1:35)

The Septuagint (LXX) translates the Hebrew of Exodus 40:34 as follows:

> [34] καὶ ἐκάλυψεν ἡ νεφέλη τὴν σκηνὴν τοῦ μαρτυρίου καὶ δόξης κυρίου ἐπλήσθη ἡ σκηνή

> וַיְכַס הֶעָנָן, אֶת-אֹהֶל מוֹעֵד; וּכְבוֹד יְהוָה, מָלֵא אֶת-הַמִּשְׁכָּן

---

[21] Pitre, Brant James. Jesus and the Jewish Roots of Mary (p. 58). The Crown Publishing Group. Kindle Edition.

[34] Then the cloud covered (וַיְכַס הֶעָנָן) (ἐκάλυψεν ἡ νεφέλη) the tent of meeting, and the glory of the LORD filled the tabernacle. (Exod 40:34)

We can see that the Septuagint translates the Hebrew phrase וַיְכַס הֶעָנָן (and the cloud covered) with the Greek phrase καὶ ἐκάλυψεν ἡ νεφέλη, while Luke uses Πνεῦμα Ἅγιον ἐπελεύσεται ἐπὶ σέ which we translate as "the Holy Spirit will come upon you." So, while Exodus 40:34 and Luke 1:35 may parallel each other still, the wording used is simply not the same. In Exodus 40:35:

וְלֹא-יָכֹל מֹשֶׁה, לָבוֹא אֶל-אֹהֶל מוֹעֵד--כִּי-שָׁכַן עָלָיו, הֶעָנָן; וּכְבוֹד יְהוָה, מָלֵא אֶת-הַמִּשְׁכָּן

καὶ οὐκ ἠδυνάσθη Μωυσῆς εἰσελθεῖν εἰς τὴν σκηνὴν τοῦ μαρτυρίου ὅτι ἐπεσκίαζεν ἐπ᾽ αὐτὴν ἡ νεφέλη καὶ δόξης κυρίου ἐπλήσθη ἡ σκηνή

[35] And Moses was not able to enter the tent of meeting because the cloud had settled on it (כִּי-שָׁכַן עָלָיו, הֶעָנָן) (ὅτι ἐπεσκίαζεν ἐπ᾽ αὐτὴν ἡ νεφέλη), and the glory of the LORD filled the tabernacle (וּכְבוֹד יְהוָה, מָלֵא אֶת-הַמִּשְׁכָּן). (Ex 40:35)

The Hebrew phrase כִּי-שָׁכַן עָלָיו, הֶעָנָן (and settled upon it, the cloud) with the Greek phrase ἐπεσκίαζεν ἐπ᾽ αὐτὴν ἡ νεφέλη (settled upon it, the cloud) has direct linguistic connection with the phrase in Luke 1:35 – "and the power of the Most High will overshadow (ἐπισκιάσει) you". The Hebrew שָׁכַן (settled) that is used in the text above, is the same root as the word מִשְׁכָּן (tabernacle). The word שכן (neighbor) and שכנה (female neighbor) are related words, but so is a later rabbinic Jewish term for God's presence, known among some Christians as *Shekeina* Glory. One can easily see the connection.

The literary and linguistic connection that many Church Fathers make that Brant Pitre refers to in his book is a valid one (Exod.40:35 and Luke 1:35), but the acknowledgment should be made that it is weakened by the lack of the corresponding phrases

(Exodus 40:34 and Luke 1:35). In other words, while the same word is used in both Exodus 40:35 (ἐπεσκίαζεν, settled/ overshadowed) and Luke 1:35 (ἐπισκιάσει, settled/ overshadowed), the argument would have been unchallengeable if the phrase (cloud covered, ἐκάλυψεν) in Exodus 40:34 also showed up in Luke 1:35. Instead Luke has something else that may or may not be an intentional parallel (the Holy Spirit will come upon you, ἐπελεύσεται).

This whole discussion is also complicated by the fact that, in the end, we may be comparing apples to oranges when we compare the Septuagint Greek to the Masoretic Hebrew text. The reason for this is that there seems to be some evidence to suggest that Jewish translators of the Septuagint had in their possession a different family of Torah manuscripts than the ones we are discussing in the corresponding Hebrew sections. So hypothetically there once might have been greater linguistic correspondence than we can see now. But be that as it may, we can only compare the texts that we have now and cannot appeal to ones that we wish we had.

Contents of the Ark

From the Catholic perspective, one of the primary reasons Mary of Nazareth is seen as the New Testament fulfillment of the Old Testament ark of the covenant lies in the fact that she bore within her - albeit for a limited time - the Word of God Himself (John 1:14) who is the Bread of Life (John 6:35) and our true High Priest (Heb 4:14-16), Christ Jesus, the King. As mentioned before, the Old Testament ark of the covenant held (according to our translations of Hebrews 9:3-4) the tablets inscribed with the Ten Commandments (God's word), samples of Manna from heaven, and Aaron's budded rod, which was once used to confirm the authority of the Levitical priesthood. While this argument from our Catholic brothers and sisters carries weight, I have reservations about accepting it and present two counterarguments.

First, Mary was pregnant with Jesus for only nine months. After Jesus' birth, I struggled to see a compelling argument for her continued status as the ark of the covenant, given that the Word of God was no longer within her. Someone could respond, however, that a mother is always a mother. Only because the baby Jesus was out of the womb at his birth, the work of the mother did not stop. In fact, it may have only begun. It would be many years before Jesus became an independent man. Naturally, it would be at the foot of the cross that Blessed Mary would have felt the full weight of her ongoing motherhood of Jesus.

Second, the nature of Jesus' ministry is so vast and encompassing that virtually any concept can be traced back to our esteemed Lord. He fulfills the roles of prophet, priest, and king, and in relation to these offices (three in one), every spiritual concept in the Hebrew Bible/Old Testament can find its fulfillment in Him.

An old anecdote may be relevant here. In Sunday school, the teacher asks children: "Dear children, what do you think it is? It's sometimes smelly. It's got four legs. It barks. It has a tail at the back. It can be a friend to people. One kid, says, I know the answer is Jesus, but it sounds like you are talking about our family dog."

To illustrate this point to you further, I want to share with you something that was brought to my attention during the review process of the book. My former student and now a colleague and a friend Song Huang pointed out to me something that I missed. Apparently, the budded rod of Aaron was never inside the ark of the covenant. This was also the case with the manna that was placed into a jar at God's command as a testimony to Israel's future generations. Thinking that all three are contained in the ark of the covenant is a misreading of Hebrews 9. Please, let me explain. The Ark of the Covenant contained exclusively the Ten Commandments and the Ten Commandments alone. We read in 1 Kings 8 (but also in 2 Chronicles 5),

> [1] Then Solomon assembled the elders of Israel and all the heads of the tribes, the leaders of the fathers' households of the sons of Israel, to King Solomon in Jerusalem, to bring up the ark of the covenant of the LORD from the city of David, that is, Zion... [4] And they brought up the ark of the LORD, the tent of meeting, and all the holy utensils which were in the tent; the priests and the Levites brought them up... [6] Then the priests brought the ark of the covenant of

the LORD to its place, into the inner sanctuary of the house, to the Most Holy Place, under the wings of the cherubim… [9] There was nothing in the ark except the two tablets of stone which Moses put there at Horeb, where the LORD made a covenant with the sons of Israel, when they came out of the land of Egypt. (1 Kings 8:1-9)

Both texts (1 Kings 8:9 and 2 Chron 5:10) are emphatic and clear. There was nothing except the Ten Commandments inside of the ark of the covenant. So why does the Epistle to the Hebrews say otherwise? We read:

[1] Now even the first covenant had regulations for divine worship and the earthly sanctuary. [2] For a tabernacle was equipped, the outer sanctuary, in which were the lampstand, the table, and the sacred bread; this is called the Holy Place. [3] Behind the second veil (μετὰ δὲ τὸ δεύτερον καταπέτασμα) there was a tabernacle which is called the Most Holy Place, [4] having a golden altar of incense and the ark of the covenant (καὶ τὴν κιβωτὸν τῆς διαθήκης) covered on all sides with gold, in (ἐν) which (ᾗ) was a golden jar holding the manna (στάμνος χρυσῆ ἔχουσα τὸ μάννα), Aaron's staff which budded (ἡ ῥάβδος Ἀαρὼν ἡ βλαστήσασα), and the tablets of the covenant (αἱ πλάκες τῆς διαθήκης) [5] and above it were the cherubim of glory overshadowing the atoning cover; but about these things we cannot now speak in detail. (Hebrews 9:1-5)

Most Christians (including me for over 25 years!), after reading Hebrews 9, have erroneously concluded that the ark of the covenant had three items inside of it, not one. But upon closer reading (and especially taking into consideration the text in 1 Kings and 2 Chronicles among others) it is very possible that the Epistle to the Hebrews does not make this claim about the contents of the Ark of the Covenant at all, but about the inner sanctum instead ("behind the second veil..." in vs. 3). It is true the sentence could have been clearer, but it wasn't.

Greek lexicographers give numerous definitions for this word (ἐν), translated as "in", including among, within the range of, near, before, in the presence of, etc.[22] It is possible, therefore, that the author of Hebrews intended to communicate that Aaron's rod, the container of manna, and the stone tablets were all in close proximity to the ark in the Most Holy Place. The stone tablets were inside the ark, while the manna and the rod were placed in front of it, as noted in Exodus 16:33-34 and Numbers 17:10. We read:

> [33] And Moses said to Aaron, "Take a jar and put a full omer of manna in it, and place it before the LORD to be kept safe throughout your generations." [34] As the LORD commanded Moses, so Aaron placed it before the Testimony, to be kept. (Ex 16:33-34)

And:

> [10] But the LORD said to Moses, "Put the staff of Aaron back in front of the testimony to be kept as a sign against the rebels, so that you may put an end to their grumblings against Me and they do not die." (Num 17:10)

From the Exodus 16 and Numbers 17 texts, it is rather obvious that both the rod of Aaron as well as the jar of manna were supposed to be placed in front/nearby/in proximity to the ark of the covenant itself. Hence the problem may lie in the translation from the Greek. This very interesting excursus into a seeming inaccuracy in the information of Hebrew 9 concerning the ark of the covenant illustrates my point. We must be very careful when it comes to our arguments about something being fulfilled in Jesus (like manna and rod), simply because almost everything (if not

---

[22] Danker, Frederick William (2000), A Greek-English Lexicon of the New Testament and Other Early Christian Literature (Chicago: University of Chicago Press), Third edition, pp. 326-330.

everything) does indeed find it ultimate fulfillment in either the person, work or teaching of Christ, the King.

This of course does not fully negate the Catholic argument that Mary is the ark of the new covenant, because just like the ark contained the word of God, so did she, if only for a short period of time. It, however, at least to my mind, weakens it further.

2 Sam 6 and Luke 1

To be able to do justice to the argument about the possibility of Luke intentionally paralleling his account in Luke 1 to the "Return of the Ark to Jerusalem" story found in 2 Samuel chapter 6, I first want to present the main argument drawn from Brant Pitre's book, from the beginning to the end, as best I understand it. I sincerely hope not to misrepresent the argument so that I can analyze it with a clear conscience. Once you consider all the points below, I will provide my own critical analysis of each one. Then you can give further thought to it and see whether you want to agree with my analysis or not. Remember, you don't have to. The important thing is not to agree, but to grow in our ability to think honestly and objectively.

So here are the five arguments in favor:

1) David "arose and went" to the hill country of Judah to bring up "the ark of God" (2 Sam 6:2). Mary "arose and went" into the hill country of Judah to visit Elizabeth (Luke 1:39).

2) David admits his unworthiness to receive the ark by exclaiming: "How can the ark of the LORD come to me?" (2 Sam 6:9). Elizabeth admits her unworthiness to receive Mary by exclaiming: "And why is this granted to me, that the mother of my Lord should come to me?" (Luke 1:43).

3) Dressed as a priest, David dances in front of the ark (2 Sam 6:14). John the Baptist – of priestly lineage – leaps in his mother's womb at the approach of Mary (Luke 1:41).

4) David "leaped" before the ark as it is brought in "with shouting" (2 Sam 6:15–16). John "leaped" in Elizabeth's womb at the sound of Mary's voice and Elizabeth cries

"with a loud shout" (Luke 1:41–42).

5)   The ark remains in the hill country, in the house of Obed-Edom, "three months" (2 Sam 6:11). Mary remains in the hill country, in Elizabeth's house, "three months" (Luke 1:56).

I imagine that the above made the same impression on you as it did on me when I first heard it. However, as I began to zoom in on each point, I realized that while this topic was interesting and indeed intriguing, some arguments were not as strong as they first seemed. Let me explain.

Point #1 in Brant Pitre's book:

David "arose and went" (וַיָּקָם וַיֵּלֶךְ) to the hill country of Judah to bring up "the ark of God" (2 Sam 6:2). Mary "arose and went" into the hill country of Judah to visit Elizabeth (Luke 1:39).

My brief evaluation:

In 2 Sam 6:2 we read:

וַיָּקָם וַיֵּלֶךְ דָּוִד, וְכָל-הָעָם אֲשֶׁר אִתּוֹ, מִבַּעֲלֵי, יְהוּדָה-לְהַעֲלוֹת מִשָּׁם,
אֵת אֲרוֹן הָאֱלֹהִים

> [2] And David rose up and went with all the people who were with him from Baale-Judah, to bring up from there the ark of God...

In Luke 1:39:

> [39] Mary having risen up (Ἀναστᾶσα) in these days and went (ἐπορεύθη) in a hurry to the hill country, to a city of Judah. Ἀναστᾶσα δὲ Μαριὰμ ἐν ταῖς ἡμέραις ταύταις ἐπορεύθη εἰς τὴν ὀρεινὴν μετὰ σπουδῆς πόλιν Ἰούδα.

In 2 Sam 6:2 in Greek Septuagint translation from Hebrew we read: καὶ ἀνέστη (rose up) καὶ ἐπορεύθη (went) Δαυιδ καὶ πᾶς ὁ λαὸς ὁ μετ' αὐτοῦ ἀπὸ τῶν ἀρχόντων Ιουδα ἐν ἀναβάσει τοῦ ἀναγαγεῖν ἐκεῖθεν τὴν κιβωτὸν τοῦ θεοῦ. Even though I am not out to find reasons not to accept suggested parallel, and I find the theory quite attractive, I cannot ignore several things that may argue against the validity of this point. First, while the words "rose up" and "went" found in 2 Sam 6:2 indeed are also found in Luke 1:39, they are not found as a phrase "and he rose up and went" as they are found in both the Hebrew (וַיָּקָם וַיֵּלֶךְ) and the Septuagint (LXX) Greek (καὶ ἀνέστη καὶ ἐπορεύθη) of 2 Sam 6:2.

Considering the fact that the Septuagint was *the* translation that the author of the Gospel of Luke would have used as his Bible (this Gospel often quotes the Septuagint), it is strange that he would not use the same phraseology *if* he really wanted to draw the literary parallel that Brant Pitre claims he did. It could be argued, that the parallel is there, but that the author of Luke did not intend it to be so obvious and, therefore, did not have a problem not to use exact phraseology in Greek from Hebrew.

Second, there are many instances in the Bible where someone "rose up" and then "went" in the same sentence, as in Luke 1:39, suggesting that these actions don't necessarily authenticate the unique nature of an event. Both the Old and New Testaments emerge from a Jewish context, employing similar Hebraic modes of expression. In other words, this doesn't prove an explicit intention from the author's perspective the way that my Catholic brothers and sisters may argue.

Third, Brant Pitre claims that both went to "the hill country of Judah", but upon a closer comparison of 2 Sam 6 and Luke 1 this does not seem to be the case. While it is true that Mary went to the hill country of Judah, this does not seem to be reflected in 2 Sam 6:2. There are different ways to translate the original Hebrew לְהַעֲלוֹת מִשָּׁם מִבַּעֲלֵי יְהוּדָה but the grammar clearly indicates the movement is not *towards* Judah, but a way from it. NASB/ESV/KJV, for example, translate it as: "from Baale-Judah, to bring up from there". There are a few translator teams that opted for some unknown reason to say that David's movement was towards Judah and not away from it. NIV has it as "went to Baalah in Judah to bring up from there" and NLT as "led them to Baalah of Judah to bring back…". What we can see here, however, is that the Hebrew of 2 Sam 6:2 is not very clear, and the argument "went to the hill country of Judah" cannot be based on this alleged linguistic connection.[23]

Point #2 in Brant Pitre's book:

David admits his unworthiness to receive the ark by exclaiming: "How can the ark of the LORD come to me?" (2 Sam 6:9). Elizabeth admits her unworthiness to receive Mary by exclaiming: "And why is this granted to me, that the mother of my Lord should come to me?" (Luke 1:43).

My brief evaluation:

The central claim here is both David and Elizabeth make a reference to the feeling of unworthiness in front of something or someone representing the Lord in a powerful way (the ark of the covenant coming to Jerusalem and pregnant Mary coming to Elizabeth). Again, here I agree that Elizabeth is indeed displaying an attitude of awe. But, unfortunately, in David's case this is again not so. We read in 2 Sam 6:6-10:

> [6] But when they came to the threshing floor of Nacon, Uzzah reached out toward the ark of God and took

---

[23] The Catholic Vulgate has this verse in 2 Kings as: [2] Surrexitque et abiit et universus populus qui erat cum eo de viris Iuda ut adducerent arcam Dei super quam invocatum est nomen Domini exercituum sedentis in cherubin super eam. (2 Kings 6:2) A somewhat direct translation of this verse is "And [David] arose and departed, and all the people who he was with *of* the men of Judah that *they were bringing/might bring (subjunctive)* the ark of God, upon which the name of the Lord of Hosts is being invoked, who sitteth over it upon the cherubims. The Latin is true to the Hebrew in the sense that it is saying David and the people with him were *departing of* ("of" is sometimes interchangeable in Latin with "from") the men of Judah. Somehow the translators of the Vulgate derived "men of" from the Hebrew word "Baalah" but nonetheless the Catholic Bible doesn't argue Brant Pitre's point either. In Luke 1:39 from the Vulgate we read: [39] *Exsurgens* autem Maria in diebus illis *abiit in* montana cum festinatione *in* civitatem Iuda. The Douay–Rheims translation of the Vulgate has this verse as: [39] And rising up, Mary in those days, departed *into* the hill country with haste *into* the city of Juda. (Luke 1:39) *Exsurgens* (from Luke) and *surrexitque* (from 2 Sam) come from the same verb *Surgo or Surgere*, meaning to raise, stand-up, ascend. *Abiit* is the second verb used in both verses and means "to depart" or "go away". The Vulgate again agrees that Mary is traveling towards the hill country as the Latin word used to indicate her direction is "in" meaning "in" or "into". It is quite clear in the Catholic Bible that these two verses don't say the same thing. (Special thanks for this insight to my friend and one of the editors of this book Jennifer Boudreau)

hold of it, for the oxen nearly upset *it*. [7] And the anger of the LORD burned against Uzzah, and God struck him down there for his irreverence; and he died there by the ark of God. [8] David became angry/displeased because of the LORD'S outburst against Uzzah (וַיִּחַר לְדָוִד, עַל אֲשֶׁר פָּרַץ יְהוָה פֶּרֶץ בְּעֻזָּה), and that place is called Perez-uzzah to this day. [9] So David was afraid of the LORD that day; and he said, "How can the ark of the LORD come to me? (וַיִּרָא דָוִד אֶת-יְהוָה, בַּיּוֹם הַהוּא וַיֹּאמֶר, אֵיךְ יָבוֹא אֵלַי אֲרוֹן יְהוָה)." [10] And David was unwilling to move the ark of the LORD into the city of David with him, but David took it aside to the house of Obed-edom the Gittite.

We read in Luke 1:42-44:

[42] And she cried out with a loud voice and said, "Blessed *are* you among women, and blessed *is* the fruit of your womb! [43] And how has it happened to me that the mother of my Lord would come to me? (και ποθεν μοι τουτο ινα ελθη η μητηρ του κυριου μου προς με) [44] For behold, when the sound of your greeting reached my ears, the baby leaped in my womb for joy.

So, while Elizabeth's and David's explanations appear very similar, their meaning is very different. Elizabeth is thankful to God, while David is angry and disappointed with him. If Brant Pitre meant in Point #2 that both David and Elizabeth felt unworthy, then perhaps this connection could stand. But even if he did not, this parallel could still hold. Sometimes Hebrew literary parallels work in an inverted way. But to me this certainly weakens the case for Luke 1 being an intentional parallel to 2 Samuel 6.

Points #3-4 in Brant Pitre's book:

3)   Dressed as a priest, David danced in front of the ark (2 Sam 6:14). John the Baptist – of priestly lineage – leapt in his mother's womb at the approach of Mary (Luke 1:41).

4) David "leaped" before the ark as it was brought in "with shouting" (2 Sam 6:15–16). John "leaped" in Elizabeth's womb at the sound of Mary's voice and Elizabeth cried "with a loud shout" (Luke 1:41–42).

My brief evaluation:

This suggested connection works beautifully. After some time, the ark of the covenant begins to bring blessings and not curses to the house of Obed-Edom the Gittite, King David is ready to bring the ark into Jerusalem. We read in 2 Samel:

> ^{12} Now it was told King David, saying, "The LORD has blessed the house of Obed-edom and all that belongs to him, on account of the ark of God." David went and brought up the ark of God from the house of Obed-edom into the city of David with gladness. ^{13} And so it was, that when the bearers of the ark of the LORD had gone six paces, he sacrificed an ox and a fatling. ^{14} And David was dancing before the LORD with all *his* might, and David was wearing a linen ephod (בַּד חָגוּר אֵפוֹד). ^{15} So David and all the house of Israel were bringing up the ark of the LORD with shouting and the sound of the trumpet. (2 Sam 6:12-15)

In Luke, we read:

> ^{5} In the days of Herod, king of Judea, there was a priest named Zechariah, of the division of Abijah; and he had a wife from the daughters of Aaron, and her name was Elizabeth. (Luke 1:5)

While David is not a Levite, he is dressed as a priest when he is welcoming the ark of the covenant into Jerusalem. Elizabeth and her unborn child rejoicing and even leaping about Mary's coming is, therefore, a valid parallel since both Elizabeth and soon-to-be John the Baptist belong to the tribe of Levi.

Point #5 in Brant Pitre's book:

The ark remains in the hill country, in the house of Obed-Edom, "three months" (2 Sam 6:11). Mary remains in the hill country, in Elizabeth's house, "three months" (Luke 1:56).

My brief evaluation:

After the Uzzah incident with him touching the ark and David's subsequent anger and distrust of the LORD, the ark remains in the home of Obed-Edom, the Gittite.

> [10] And David was unwilling to move the ark of the LORD into the city of David with him, but David took it aside to the house of Obed-Edom the Gittite (בֵּית עֹבֵד-אֱדֹם הַגִּתִּי).
> [11] The ark of the LORD remained in the house of Obed-Edom the Gittite for three months (שְׁלֹשָׁה חֳדָשִׁים), and the LORD blessed Obed-Edom and all his household. (2 Sam 6:10-11).

Note the amount of time it remained there - three months. In Luke 1:56 we read:

> [56] Mary stayed with her about three months, and *then* returned to her home. [56] Ἔμεινεν δὲ Μαριὰμ σὺν αὐτῇ ὡς (as/about) μῆνας τρεῖς καὶ ὑπέστρεψεν εἰς τὸν οἶκον αὐτῆς. [56] Dwelt then Mary with her about months three and returned to the home of her (a literal translation into English).

Note that while the timeframe of three months is mentioned in both stories, the first use does not have any qualifying words like "about", but the second text adds uses "about" before "three months." It may or may not be important. One can argue that the use in Hebrew may be approximate; after all, I doubt that they counted actual days. It would be logical to assume that three months there were approximated. Let us again consult the Septuagint. Perhaps, there we can find a more concrete hint at the approximation of three months. In 2 Sam 6:11, we read: "And the ark of the Lord lodged in the house of Abeddara the Gethite three months (μῆνας τρεῖς), and the Lord blessed all the house of Abeddara, and all his possessions."

The Septuagint translates the Hebrew regarding three months without any obvious approximation. This does not mean that in 2 Sam 6:11, the three months were not approximated, but it does mean that it is unlikely that Luke is drawing an intentional parallel between the two accounts. The question should still be asked: is it possible for Luke 1 to draw on 2 Sam 6 without the use of precise language (three months vs. *about* three months)? It is certainly possible. But what is more likely: is the presence of "three months" in both stories a case of intentional parallelism or just coincidence? It is impossible to say for sure. Having considered all the five points presented above, it seems that Brant Pitre's hypothesis is rather weak. So, while I remain open to testing the Catholic position on Mary, I feel that the burden of proof rests with our Catholic brothers and sisters.

Reappearance of the Ark

Stephen Langton, the Archbishop of Canterbury from 1207 until 1228, is credited with the creation of the Bible's chapter divisions we use today The Wycliffe English Bible, published in 1382, was the first to use this chapter framework, which has been adopted by almost all subsequent Bible translations. The verse divisions in the Hebrew Old Testament were implemented by a Jewish rabbi named Nathan in 1448. The New Testament was first segmented into standard numbered verses by Robert Estienne, also known as Stephanus, in 1555. Stephanus' verse divisions for the Old Testament were largely influenced by Nathan's work. Beginning with the Geneva Bible, Stephanus' chapter and verse divisions have been incorporated into almost all Bible versions.

Despite a few instances of suboptimal chapter breaks that disrupt the content flow, the chapter and verse divisions generally serve as beneficial navigational tools. Without them, we would have trouble agreeing that we are reading and discussing a particular portion of a particular Biblical book. Our Catholic brothers and sisters will note an unfortunate section break i⸱ Bible pertaining to Mary. It is found in the Book of Revf⸴ part of this study, we have already discussed Revlatiⸯ

vision of a heavenly Woman Clothed with the Sun. In Revelation 11-12 we read:

> [19] And the temple of God which is in heaven was opened; and the ark of His covenant appeared in His temple, and there were flashes of lightning and sounds and peals of thunder, and an earthquake, and a great hailstorm. [12:1] A great sign appeared in heaven: a woman clothed with the sun, and the moon under her feet, and on her head a crown of twelve stars, [2] and she was pregnant… and she gave birth to a Son, a male, who is going to rule all the nations with a rod of iron; and her Child was caught up to God and to His throne. (Rev 11:19-12:2)

Here we can clearly see that one vision flows into another. First, the ark of the covenant appears in the heavenly temple, then immediately after the great sign in heaven appears – the Woman Clothed with the Sun. The question then becomes, are these closely related visions making the artificial chapter break illegitimate? Do they refer to one and the same person, the Virgin Mary? Or, does Revelation 12 refer to Mary (Rev 12:1-2), and the ark of the covenant vision in Rev 11:19 refer to something else? I think there are other examples that could be cited to strengthen a Catholic position from Revelation. Take for example, Revelation 5:

> [5:2] And I saw a strong angel proclaiming with a loud voice, "Who is worthy to open the scroll and to break its seals?" [3] And no one in heaven or on the earth or under the earth was able to open the scroll or to look into it. [4] Then I began to weep greatly because no one was found worthy to open the scroll or to look into it. [5] And one of the elders said to me, "Stop weeping; behold, the Lion that is from the tribe of Judah, the Root of David, has overcome so as to be able to open the scroll and its seven seals." [6] And I saw between the throne (with the four living creatures) and the elders a Lamb standing, as if slaughtered… (Rev 5:1-6)

Interestingly, John does not see the Lion from the Tribe of Judah; he hears him (more particularly, he hears *about* him). Then the vision/s progresses and he comes to see the Lamb, as if slain. Does the Lion of Judah and the Lamb that was slain refer to two different things/people/persons? No. In fact, both visions refer only to the Messiah Jesus. Also, consider another example, the relationship between the 144,000 Israelites (Rev 7:4-8) and the multinational crowd of worshipers of Israel's God in Christ (Rev 7:9). We first read: And I heard the number of those who were sealed: 144,000, sealed from every tribe of the sons of Israel... (Rev 7:4) Then we read:

> [9] After these things I looked, and behold, a great
> multitude which no one could count, from every nation
> and all the tribes, peoples, and languages, standing
> before the throne and before the Lamb, clothed
> in white robes, and palm branches were in their
> hands... (Rev 7:9)

Here too, we see the same exact dynamic of hearing one thing but seeing another. Is it possible these two visions also refer to one and the same group of people - believers of Israel's God who remain faithful unto the end? I think the answer must be a tentative yes. So, then the Catholics should argue (I don't really know if they do, I've never seen this argument presented) that since we have several examples of this kind of dual vision referring to one and the same thing then it means that the vision in Revelation 11 (Ark of the covenant in the Temple) and Revelation 12 (Woman Clothed in the Sun) could in fact be referring to one and the same thing.

Lost Ark

We will now investigate this argument as it may link the Woman Clothed with the Sun with the ark of the covenant. In Rev 11:19 we read:

> [19] And the temple of God which is in heaven was
> opened, and the ark of His covenant appeared in His

temple, and there were flashes of lightning and sounds and peals of thunder, and an earthquake, and a great hailstorm. (Rev 11:19)

In Revelation, the open temple is connected to the very idea of the presence of God in judgment and mercy, to which the presence of the ark of the covenant also testifies. But there is something else truly intriguing here. The Bible never discusses the Ark of the Covenant (אֲרוֹן הַבְּרִית; *aron haberit*) being in heaven, unless of course, it was the archetype of the early ark that Moses saw (Ex 25:9, 40). The only ark of the covenant ever known to the Israelites was the ark in the earthly Tabernacle and, later, in the Jerusalem Temple. The Ark of the Covenant is presumed to have been destroyed by Nebuzaradan (a high official of King Nebuchadnezzar II) in his razing of Jerusalem and burning the Temple to the ground (2 Kgs 25:8–10). However, in 2 Maccabees 2:4-8, we read that Jeremiah retrieves and then hides the ark in a secret cave on Mt. Nebo[24]:

> It was also in the same document that the prophet, having received an oracle, ordered that the tent and the ark should follow with him and that he went out to the mountain where Moses had gone up and had seen the inheritance of God. Jeremiah came and found a cave-dwelling, and he brought there the tent and the ark and the altar of incense; then he sealed up the entrance. Some of those who followed him came up intending to mark the way but could not find it. When Jeremiah learned of it, he rebuked them and declared, "The place shall remain unknown until God gathers His people together again and shows his mercy. Then the Lord will disclose these things, and the glory of the Lord and the cloud will appear, as they were shown in the case of Moses and as Solomon asked that the place should be specially consecrated." (2 Macc 2:4-8 NRSV)

---

[24] Robert H. Mounce, *The Book of Revelation*: New International Commentary on the New Testament, Kindle Edition (Grand Rapids, Eerdmans, 1975), 228.

The account of Jeremiah's secret safeguarding of the Ark of the Covenant offers an alluring addition to its historical enigma—a narrative that bridges the gap between the loss of this sacred artifact and its unexpected but symbolic reappearance in the apocalyptic visions of Revelation. To the devout and scholarly alike, this passage from 2 Maccabees injects both hope and mystery into the Ark's lore, suggesting a divine reservation for a time of future grace. Moreover, the disappearance and subsequent heavenly sighting underline a theological motif found throughout scripture, where sacred objects and places often transcend their physical existence, pointing towards a higher reality. The hiddenness of the Ark serves not only as a testament to God's past revelations to Moses and Solomon but also as a promise of a future unveiling in line with God's redemptive plan—a celestial Ark as both a memorial of covenant and a harbinger of mercy.

In concluding this section, I can see the case that could be made about Mary being the new ark of the New Covenant. Is it possible? Yes. Is it probable? I am still not convinced.

Concluding Reflections

Finding Common Ground in Devotion

The importance of examining the Jewish roots of historical figures is undeniable, as evidenced by the scholarship on both Jesus and Paul. Similarly, delving into the Jewishness of Mary provides profound insights into her role and portrayal within the Gospels. The Gospel of Luke meticulously depicts Mary of Nazareth as a devoutly observant Jew, highlighting her and Joseph's adherence to Torah-based practices. This includes the circumcision and purification of Jesus, presenting Him at the Temple, and partaking in the annual Passover pilgrimage. Such depictions are not merely anecdotal but serve as a testament to their unwavering dedication to the Torah and Jewish traditions. Luke, like the other Gospels, paints a vivid picture of their commitment, offering a window into the deeply rooted Jewish customs that shaped their lives and, consequently, the early Christian narrative.

Understanding Mary's Jewishness is crucial as it bridges the so-called Old and New Testaments, providing continuity and a richer context to the biblical narrative. Additionally, it reconnects the holy family narrative to Second Temple Judaism/s in its many forms. This exploration allows for a more nuanced comprehension of the Gospels, where Mary's actions and faithfulness are seen as part of a larger, divinely orchestrated plan. Her unwavering adherence to the Jewish faith underscores the importance of these traditions and offers a template of devotion that transcends time. By appreciating these roots, modern readers can gain a more holistic understanding of the cultural and religious milieu that shaped the early Christian faith and its key figures.

Fostering Unity Across Beliefs

The study of Mary's role and heritage should lead both Catholics and Protestants to a greater appreciation of the nuanced evidence, inviting humility in theological discourses. This realization necessitates a significant softening of denominational pride and a cessation of mutual demonization. The pursuit of humility and love must supersede long-standing biases, allowing for constructive dialogue that transcends doctrinal divides. In this spirit, examining Mary's Jewish background and her depiction in the Gospels can serve as a common ground for fostering ecumenical dialogue. It encourages believers to focus on shared beliefs and values, promoting a culture of respect and understanding.

Such unity is not just an idealistic goal but a practical necessity in a world increasingly fragmented by religious and ideological differences. By coming together to study and appreciate Mary's role, Catholics and Protestants can build bridges, fostering a sense of community and mutual respect. This unity can lead to collaborative efforts in addressing broader social and ethical issues, demonstrating the power of faith in uniting rather than dividing. In essence, Mary's story becomes a catalyst for healing and reconciliation, urging believers to transcend their differences and work towards common goals rooted in love and mutual respect.

Appreciating Mary's Unique Role

In Protestant realms, where Mary's role is often underrecognized, it is essential to acknowledge the uniqueness of her position within the Biblical narrative. Described as "blessed among women," Mary's journey and her designation as the mother of Jesus confer upon her a special status within the annals of faith. Yet, the depth of Catholic perspectives on Mary may be unfamiliar to many Protestants, revealing an unintentional theological isolation. To serve God meaningfully and to foster a robust spiritual life, one must remain open to diverse viewpoints without necessarily accepting them. This openness to exploration is equally critical for Catholics, cultivating a well-rounded understanding.

Mary's role extends beyond her motherhood; she is a symbol of faith, obedience, and devotion. Her acceptance of God's will, despite the personal and societal challenges it entailed, offers a profound example for all believers. By recognizing and appreciating this, Protestants can enrich their spiritual lives, drawing inspiration from Mary's example. Meanwhile, Catholics can benefit from understanding Protestant perspectives, fostering a more inclusive and comprehensive view of Mary that transcends doctrinal boundaries. This mutual appreciation can lead to a deeper, more enriched faith experience, where believers from different traditions find common ground in their reverence for Mary.

Balancing Perspectives

Although Catholic theology might emphasize positive Biblical evidence for Mary's significance, it tends to overlook the more subtle, sometimes challenging passages, such as those in Mark's Gospel that downplay familial ties. The scarcity of Marian references outside of Luke-Acts hints at a less pronounced focus across the New Testament. The inclination to use one's interpretive lens as a universal tool must be tempered with a conscientious and balanced examination of scripture. This book aims to demonstrate that an objective approach to such study is both possible and fruitful, allowing the evidence to lead to its natural conclusions.

A balanced perspective requires acknowledging both the strengths and limitations of one's theological tradition. For Catholics, this means recognizing the profound reverence for Mary while also considering the broader scriptural context. For Protestants, it involves appreciating Mary's unique role without dismissing the depth of Catholic tradition. Such a balanced approach fosters a more comprehensive understanding of Mary, allowing her story to inform and inspire a more unified Christian faith. This balanced examination encourages believers to approach scripture with humility and openness, letting the evidence guide their understanding rather than preconceived notions.

In conclusion, the study of Mary's Jewish roots, her role in the Gospels, and the varying theological perspectives across denominations offer a rich tapestry of insights. By embracing this complexity and striving for unity and balance, believers can deepen their faith, foster mutual respect, and work towards a more harmonious and inclusive Christian community. This journey of understanding and appreciation not only enriches personal faith but also strengthens the collective witness of the Christian tradition in the world.

REQUEST

Dear reader, may I ask you for a favor? If you are enjoyed this book, would you take three minutes of your time and provide encouraging feedback to other people about this book? Look up "The Jewish Roots of Mary" on Amazon.com and write a brief review! After that, please drop me a personal note and let me know that you did so - dr.eli.israel@gmail.com. Thank you so much for your support and encouragement!

In His Grace,

Dr. Eli Lizorkin-Eyzenberg

Appendix I: Mary in Prayers

Theological explorations of the kind that I feature here may sadly only be familiar to a relatively small number of people within the Catholic community. That is why I have chosen to examine several prayers together with you that are representative of many others. These prayers were selected because they are well-known, and cover multiple aspects, allowing us to explore the liturgical and practical implications of the Catholic views of Mary. In this chapter, my comments will be brief, and the value of the following text lies mainly in the ready display of the actual prayers that those who believe in communicating with Mary use most often. It is important for you and me to have actual texts of the prayers before us. Since they reflect, in very clear ways, how believers perceive Mary in their theologies. I chose to dedicate this chapter to several Catholic prayers. I used modern English translations so that we can better grasp their basic ideas better.

Sub tuum praesidium (Under Your Protection)
We flee to your protection,
holy Mother of God.
Do not ignore our prayers in our time of need,
but from every danger free us always,
O glorious, O blessed Virgin.

"Sub tuum praesidium" is a prayer that dates to the third century. Its main ideas revolve around seeking protection and help from the Virgin Mary since she gave birth to God incarnate, Jesus. We can see here that the role of Mary as the Mother of God (Theotokos) is deeply connected to the high Christology held by Catholics. The prayer acknowledges Mary's role as a powerful intercessor and asks for her assistance in times of trouble and danger. It emphasizes the belief in Mary's motherly love and her ability to provide comfort and refuge. The prayer also acknowledges the vulnerability and frailty of human beings and their need for divine help. Overall, "Sub tuum praesidium " expresses a deep sense of trust and reliance on the protection of the Virgin Mary.

Ave Maria (Hail Mary)
Hail Mary, full of grace, the Lord is with you;
Blessed are you among women,
and blessed is the fruit of your womb, Jesus.
Holy Mary, Mother of God,
pray for us sinners,
now and at the hour of our death.
Amen.

"Ave Maria" is a prayer that holds significant importance in Catholic and Christian traditions. The main ideas in this prayer revolve around first, honoring and second, seeking the intercession of the Virgin Mary. It begins with the salutation "Ave Maria" (Hail Mary) and acknowledges Mary as being full of grace and having a special presence of the Lord, while being blessed more than any other woman. Both are words that are reanimated from Gabriel's and Elizabeth's encounters with Mary. The prayer expresses reverence for Mary's role as the mother of Jesus and seeks her prayers for guidance, protection, and mercy. It acknowledges the incarnation of Jesus and asks for her intercession throughout the totality of believer's life. "Ave Maria" is a prayer that gives to Mary the honor that is due to her from the people of God and requests her holy intercession on behalf of a redeemed, but broken humanity.

Salve Regina (Hail Queen)
Hail, holy Queen, mother of mercy,
our life, our sweetness, and our hope.
To you do we cry,

121

poor banished children of Eve.
To you do we send up our sighs
mourning and weeping in this vale of tears.
Turn, then, most gracious Advocate,
your eyes of mercy towards us;
and after this exile
show us the blessed fruit of your womb, Jesus.
O clement, O loving, O sweet Virgin Mary.

"Salve Regina" is a widely known prayer-hymn in Catholic liturgy. The main ideas of this hymn revolve around seeking the intercession and protection of the Virgin Mary. It begins with the salutation "Salve Regina" (Hail, Queen) and acknowledges Mary as the Queen of Heaven. The hymn expresses a sense of longing and supplication, asking for Mary's mercy, compassion, and guidance as the mother of all humanity. It recognizes the challenges and difficulties of life and seeks Mary's help in finding comfort and relief. The prayer views Mary as a powerful advocate in heaven on behalf of sinners who are saved by the grace of God through Christ. It requests that Mary continue to intercede for believers throughout their lives and help the praying community to see Jesus in all His beauty and fullness. Thus, we can see that this prayer to Mary ultimately seeks her intercession and a clearer vision of Jesus.

Alma Redemptoris Mater
Mother of Christ! Hear thou thy people's cry,
Star of the deep, and portal of the sky!
Mother of him who thee from nothing made,
Sinking we strive, and call to thee for aid:
Oh, by that joy which Gabriel brought to thee,
Thou Virgin first and last, let us thy mercy see.

"Alma Redemptoris Mater" is a Latin prayer-hymn that holds a special place in Catholic liturgy. Its name translates to "Loving Mother of the Redeemer," and it is commonly sung during the Advent and Christmas seasons. The hymn is a prayer to the Virgin Mary, acknowledging her role as the mother of Jesus Christ and the source of hope and salvation for humanity. Perhaps most striking and theologically poignant line is "*Mother of him who thee from nothing made*", highlighting Mary as Theotokos and its paradox. The lyrics express reverence and devotion, seeking Mary's intercession and protection. "Alma Redemptoris Mater" is not only a beautiful musical composition but also a powerful expression of faith and a reminder of Mary's central role in the Catholic narrative.

Appendix II: Could Luke be Jewish?

All four canonical gospels are, technically speaking, anonymous documents. It is only later tradition that ascribes to them their formal current titles/authorship as Matthew, Mark, Luke and John. There is nothing in the Gospel of Luke that can clearly identify someone named Luke as its author. Ironically this stands in sharp contrast with the non-canonical gospels, which usually go out of their way to identify various New Testament figures as their authors in order to gain credibility. The canonical Gospels, like most other books of the Hebrew Bible, do no such thing. We really don't know if a person named Luke, who accompanied Paul, was the same person who wrote the books of the Bible we call The Gospel of Luke and the Acts of the Apostles. But be that as it may, for the purpose of reference, we all, including myself, refer to the author of the Gospel of Luke simply as Luke, and accordingly, I will follow this custom in this essay. My story begins almost 20 years ago in a Seminary class in Central Florida. Back then I was convinced that Luke was not Jewish.

Why? Well… largely because everyone I knew believed that was so. The idea that Luke may have been Jewish was treated only jokingly: "You know… How can people say that Luke was not Jewish, he was a doctor!!!"

In this article I have only one goal – to show that the idea of Luke being Jewish is not as radical an idea as may have been previously thought. My clear and express purpose is not to prove that Luke was Jewish – that I believe is unachievable – but to clearly show why I believe that 1) Luke being a Gentile is an unfounded proposition and 2) there is in fact a real possibility that Luke was in fact either born a Jew or a proselyte convert to Judaism for many years.

Inconclusive arguments against Luke being Jewish

Like most people, I did not question it – until that fateful Monday morning when I was listening to a seminary lecture. The professor, who incidentally authored around 40 books and loved the Jewish people dearly, took up the topic of "Luke not being Jewish." At first, I said: "Oh no, more of the same again". But as I began to listen to the arguments of this very learned man as to why we know for sure that Luke was not Jewish, I remember clearly telling myself: "The arguments are weak and inconclusive. In fact, they make no sense."

Examples of the arguments included: 'Luke writing in better Greek than the authors of other gospels' – as if no Jew in the Roman Empire had an excellent command of the Greek language; 'Luke being a Greek name' – as if some Jews of that time did not also use Greek names, alongside their Jewish ones, like John Mark (Yohanan Markus) or Saul Paul (Shaul Paulus) for that matter; and, 'Luke displayed much interest in the nations of the world' – as if Jewish thought was not, by that time, full of visions of the Nations coming to worship the God of Israel. I found only one argument he presented worthy of any attention, and I will discuss that later and show that on examination this argument is also inconclusive and may be countered by a stronger argument pointing to the Jewishness of Luke.

Inconclusive arguments for Luke being Jewish

As I went about my life, occasionally, I would raise this question in my head and look around for some possibilities. There were a few brave souls who argued for the Jewishness of Luke, but their arguments, much like the arguments of the traditional camp, sounded unconvincing at best. Among them were arguments such as: "Luke was Jewish because all Scriptures had to come from the Jews." (Rom. 3:1-2) – As if Luke could not have been a Gentile God-fearer, fully conversant with the Jewish ways of life and thinking of his time; "Luke was Jewish because he had a detailed knowledge of the Temple Levitical operations." (Luke 1:8-20) – as if this, like other subjects Luke researched, could not have been borrowed knowledge from a priestly source; and "Luke was Jewish because he had meetings with Mary, Jesus' mother, and described her very thoughts." (Luke 2:19, 51) – as if each time a Biblical author ever described something, he had to have had a personal encounter with the person he was describing, and as if the idea that Mary would agree to talk to a Gentile God-fearer was out of the question.

Enough said! As you can see, I am not persuaded, either by those who say Luke was Jewish, or by those who say no, he was not. It is at this point that an argument could be made that, since all the arguments are unconvincing, the burden of proof belongs with those who say that Luke was the only non-Israelite author among all the other writers of the Bible. There is some rationale here of course, but for the time being, I would like to treat this argument as a "hit below the belt" – to use imagery from a boxing ring.

I will now present for your consideration what I believe to be the only argument that can be legitimately used to claim that Luke was not Jewish. I will then counter that by presenting an argument to show that Luke may indeed have been Jewish.

Argument against Luke being Jewish

To my mind, the only argument worth its salt that can be presented to claim that Luke was not Jewish, is an argument concerning Colossians 4:7-18, especially verses 10-11. There we read:

> 7 As to all my affairs, Tychicus, our beloved brother
> and faithful servant and fellow bond-servant in the
> Lord, will bring you information. 8 For I have sent him
> to you for this very purpose, that you may know about
> our circumstances and that he may encourage your
> hearts; 9 and with him Onesimus, our faithful and
> beloved brother, who is one of your number. They will
> inform you about the whole situation here. 10
> Aristarchus, my fellow prisoner, sends you his
> greetings; and also Barnabas's cousin Mark (about
> whom you received instructions; if he comes to you,
> welcome him); 11 and also Jesus who is called Justus;

126

these are the only fellow workers for the Kingdom of God who are from the circumcision, and they have proved to be an encouragement to me. 12 Epaphras, who is one of your number, a bondslave of Jesus Christ, sends you his greetings, always laboring earnestly for you in his prayers, that you may stand perfect and fully assured in all the will of God.13 For I testify for him that he has a deep concern for you and for those who are in Laodicea and Hierapolis. 14 Luke, the beloved physician, sends you his greetings, and also Demas. 15 Greet the brethren who are in Laodicea and also Nympha and the church that is in her house.16 When this letter is read among you, have it also read in the church of the Laodiceans; and you, for your part read my letter that is coming from Laodicea. 17 Say to Archippus, "Take heed to the ministry which you have received in the Lord, that you may fulfill it." 18 I, Paul, write this greeting with my own hand. Remember my imprisonment. Grace be with you. (Colossians 4:7-18)

The central idea in this argument is that, in verses 10-11, when Paul mentions several people, classifying them as the only workers with him from the circumcision (meaning those who are Jewish/Israelite), he does not mention Luke. In fact, he does mention Luke in this letter, but in a separate place and only later, thus declaring Luke as not being part of those who labor with Paul who are "of the circumcision" (or so it is argued!).

Here is why I don't believe that this is the only way to look at this text. First of all, this is part of a letter and not a systematic theological treatment of the matter, and as such it follows the normal dynamic of letter writing. We know that Paul did not write his own letters but usually dictated them, signing and approving them at the end. (See Rom.16:22; Col. 4:18; Gal.6:11.)

If we write or dictate a letter, we might write something to make our point, and then, if we have forgotten to include an important detail, we may add a p.s. (a postscript or that which comes after the writing), and even a p.p.s (a post-postscript, that which comes after that which comes after the writing). Since the Letter to the Colossians is just that – a letter – it is possible that the reason Luke was not included earlier is that Paul either forgot to include him and remembered only afterward or did not include him there because he was a doctor and not a member of his teaching team. In other words, the argument that says that this separate mention clearly sets Luke apart from Paul's kinsmen is unsound, simply because it tries to extract too much mileage from this text. It cannot prove what it sets out to prove. It only allows it as one possible reading of this textual unit.

Argument for Luke being Jewish

The argument I find very interesting as to the possibility that Luke was Jewish, is twofold: First, the name Luke is a strange name. It is strange because it rarely appears outside of the New Testament collection, although we have a vast number of documents in Greek mentioning thousands of Greek names. So we are justified in asking an additional question: 'What if Luke is not his full name? What if Paul does here with Luke the same thing he does with his friend Demas?' Demas, who is mentioned together with Luke in Colossians 4:14, is in all probability a diminutive of Demitrius – what we would call a nickname. If this is so, then Luke may also be a diminutive version of a Greek name that is very well-attested in Greek literature. That name is Lucius. In English, Luke and Lucius have only 2 letters in common, but in Greek, they share five letters (Λουκᾶς and Λούκιος). In fact, in Greek, they are almost one and the same name.

Second, now that we have established the possibility that Luke and Lucius may refer to the same person, let us consider a text that links someone named Lucius to Paul's own kinsmen! In Paul's letter to the Romans, we read:

> 17 Now I urge you, brethren, keep your eye on those who cause dissensions and hindrances contrary to the teaching which you learned, and turn away from them. 18 For such men are slaves, not of our Lord Christ but of their own appetites; and by their smooth and flattering speech they deceive the hearts of the unsuspecting. 19 For the report of your obedience has reached to all; therefore I am rejoicing over you, but I

want you to be wise in what is good and innocent in
what is evil. 20 The God of peace will soon crush
Satan under your feet. The grace of our Lord Jesus be
with you. 21 Timothy my fellow worker greets you,
and so do Lucius and Jason and Sosipater, my
kinsmen. 22 I, Tertius, who write this letter, greet you
in the Lord. (Rom.16:17-23)

Notably, Paul, through his scribe Tertius (vs. 22), links
Timothy, Jason, Sosipater together with Lucius by calling them my
kinsmen! (vs. 21) If Luke and Lucius were one and the same
person, the first being a diminutive of the second, then we may
have here a very interesting case that might not prove the
Jewishness of Luke, but does succeed to offset the Colossians 4
claim. The purpose of this essay is not to prove the Jewishness of
Luke, which probably cannot be achieved conclusively in any case
due to lack of data. Instead, its purpose was to suggest a somewhat
more tempered and careful assessment that could be summarized
as follows:

The absence of proof is not proof of absence. There are no
serious reasons to continue to claim that Luke was a Gentile.
Moreover, discussion about whether the author of the Gospel of
Luke was or was not Jewish is important because despite
inconclusive evidence about his own Jewishness, his Jewish
connection is actually not at all in doubt. In some way, whether he
was ethnically a Jew or Gentile is indeed irrelevant. The most
important question is if he was a Gentile, what kind of Gentile was
he? I propose that all available evidence shows convincingly (to
me) that if he was not a Jew, he was someone who was deeply
impacted by the Jewish faith, culture, and history of the Jewish
people around him.

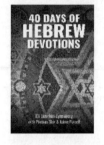
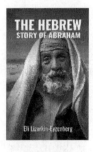

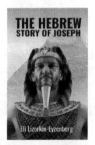

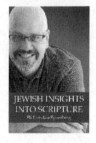

For Further Reading

Bailey, J.L. (1987). Josephus' Portrayal of the Matriarchs. In L.H. Feldman & G. Hata (Eds.), Josephus, Judaism and Christianity (pp. 94-147). Detroit: Wayne State University Press.

Bakhos, C. (2016). The Family of Abraham in Genesis Rabbah. In S.K. Gribetz, D. Grossberg, M. Himmelfarb, & P. Schäfer (Eds.), Genesis Rabbah in Text and Context (pp. 115-129). Tübingen: Mohr Siebeck.

Bauer, J. (1999). The Essential Mary Handbook. Liguori, MO: Liguori Publications.

Beattie, T. (2002). God's Mother, Eve's Advocate. London: Continuum.

Boss, Sarah Jane, ed. (2007) Mary: The Complete Resource. New York: Oxford University Press.

Buber, S. (1899). Midrasch Echa Rabbati. Vilna: Romm.

Braaten, Carl E., and Robert W. Jenson, eds. (2004) Mary: Mother of God. Grand Rapids: Eerdmans.

Brown, R.E. (1982). Mary in the New Testament and in Catholic Life. New York: Jesuits of US and Canada.

Carroll, M.P. (1986). The Cult of the Virgin Mary. Princeton, NJ: Princeton University Press.

Crawford, S.W. (2015). 'There is Much Wisdom in Her': The Matriarchs in the Qumran Library. In S. Ackerman, C.E. Carter, & B.A. Nakhai (Eds.), Celebrate Her for the Fruit of Her Hands: Essays in Honor of Carol L. Meyers (pp. 133-151). Winona Lake: Eisenbrauns.

Danker, F.W. (2000). A Greek-English Lexicon of the New Testament and Other Early Christian Literature (3rd ed.). Chicago, IL: University of Chicago Press.

Elizondo, V.P. (1980). La Morentita: Evangelizer of the Americas. San Antonio, TX: Mexican American Cultural Center.

Ehrlich, U. (2007). The Ancestors' Prayers for the Salvation of Israel in

Early Rabbinic Thought. In A. Gerhards & C. Leonhard (Eds.), Jewish and Christian Liturgy and Worship: New Insights Into Its History and Interaction (pp. 247-256). Leiden: Brill.

Ford-Grabowsky, M. (2005). Spiritual Writing on Mary: Annotated and Explained. Woodstock, VT: Skylight Paths Publishing.

Gambero, Luigi. Mary and the Fathers of the Church: The Blessed Virgin Mary in Patristic Thought, trans. Thomas Buffer. (1999) San Francisco: Ignatius.

Gebara, I. & Bingemer, M.C. (1989). Mary: Mother of God and Mother of the Poor. New York: Orbis Books.

Gribetz, S.K. (2018). "Zekhut Imahot: Mothers, Fathers, and Ancestral Merit in Rabbinic Sources." Journal for the Study of Judaism in the Persian, Hellenistic, and Roman Period 49, no. 2: 263–96.

Haffner, P. (2004). The Mystery of Mary. Chicago, IL: LTP.

Hahn, Scott. Hail, Holy Queen (2001). The Crown Publishing Group. Kindle Edition.

Haskell, H. (2012). The Death of Rachel and the Kingdom of Heaven: Jewish Engagement with Christian Themes in Sefer ha-Zohar. Journal of Medieval Religious Cultures, 38, 1-31.

Himmelfarb, M. (1998). The Mother of the Messiah in the Talmud Yerushalmi and Sefer Zerubbabel. In P. Schäfer (Ed.), The Talmud Yerushalmi and Graeco-Roman Culture (pp. 369-389). Tübingen: Mohr Siebeck.

Himmelfarb, M. (2008). The Ordeals of Abraham: Circumcision and the 'Aqedah' in Origen, the Mekhilta, and Genesis Rabbah. Henoch, 30, 289-310.

Johnson, Mary E. (2007). Miriam: A Historical Analysis of the Jewish Mother of Jesus. New Haven and London: Yale University Press.

Goldberg, David. (2002). The Virgin Mary in Jewish-Christian Polemics. New York: Routledge.

Levi, Jonathan. (2011). Mary's Influence on Medieval Jewish-Christian Dialogue. Oxford: Oxford University Press.

Stern, Rebecca. (2008). The Virgin Mary in Jewish Thought: A Comparative Study. Chicago, IL: University of Chicago Press.

Schwartz, Rachel. (2003). The Controversial Mary: Jewish-Christian Perspectives. New York: Oxford University Press.

Rosenberg, Joshua. (2013). Mary's Role in Jewish-Christian Discourse: A Critical Examination. San Francisco: Jossey-Bass.

Levy, Sarah. (2012). Mary: An Intellectual History of Jewish-Christian Perspectives. Boston, MA: Beacon Press.

Fisher, Simon. (2015). The Impact of Mary on Jewish-Christian Relations: A Scholarly Overview. Ithaca, NY: Cornell University Press.

Stein, Rachel. (2018). Mary's Influence on Medieval Jewish Thought: A Comprehensive Study. Cambridge: Cambridge University Press.

Cohen, Jacob. (2006). The Virgin Mary in Jewish-Christian Controversy: An In-Depth Analysis. New York: Palgrave Macmillan.

Levi, David. (2011). Mary: A Comparative Study of Jewish-Christian Interpretations. London: Taylor & Francis.

Steinberg, Sarah. (2019). The Legacy of Mary in Jewish-Christian Relations: A Scholarly Perspective. Cambridge: Cambridge University Press.

Kaunfer, A.H. (1995). Who Knows Four? The 'Imahot' in Rabbinic Judaism. Judaism, 44(1), 94-103.

Lieber, L.S. (2016). Stage Mothers: Performing the Matriarchs in Genesis Rabbah and Yannai. In S.K. Gribetz, D. Grossberg, M. Himmelfarb, & P. Schäfer (Eds.), Genesis Rabbah in Text and Context (pp. 155-173). Tübingen: Mohr Siebeck.

Liddell, Henry George, Robert Scott, and Henry Stuart Jones. A Greek-English Lexicon. 9th ed. with revised supplement. Oxford: Clarendon, 1996.

Macquarrie, J. (1990). Mary for All Christians. Grand Rapids, MI: William B. Eerdmans Publishing Company.

Marmorstein, A. (1968). The Doctrine of Merits in Old Rabbinical Literature. New York: Ktav Publishing House.

Moloney, F. (1988). Mary: Woman and Mother. Collegeville, MN: Liturgical Press.

Najman, H. (2014). Losing the Temple and Recovering the Future: An Analysis of 4 Ezra. Cambridge: Cambridge University Press.

Niehoff, M. (2005). Mother and Maiden, Sister and Spouse: Sarah in Philonic Midrash. Harvard Theological Review, 97, 413-444.

O'Carroll, Michael. Theotokos: A Theological Encyclopedia of the Blessed Virgin Mary (1982). Dublin: Dominican Publications.

Pelikan, J. (1998). Mary Through the Centuries: Her Place in the History of Culture. New Haven, CT: Yale University Press.

Perry, N. & Echeverria, L. (1988). Under the Heel of Mary. London/New York: Routledge.

Pitre, B.J. (2018). Jesus and the Jewish Roots of Mary. The Crown Publishing Group.

Pope John Paul II. (1987). Encyclical Letter: Mother of the Redeemer. Boston, MA: St. Paul Books & Media.

Ramon, E. (2006). The Matriarchs and the Torah of 'Hesed' (Lovingkindness). Nashim, 10, 154-177.

Rosenberg, M. (2017). Mediating Mothers: Rachel(s) and Mary as Jewish Intercessors. Paper presented at the annual meeting of the Association for Jewish Studies.

Sered, S.S. (1996). Our Mother Rachel. In A. Sharma & K. Young (Eds.), Annual Review of Women in World Religions (pp. 1-20). Albany: State University of New York Press.

Shacham-Rosby, C. (2011). From His Place He Heard Rachel's Prayer And Remembered Her: Rachel the Matriarch in Early Palestinian Midrash and Piyyut from the Byzantine Era and her Role in the Jewish-Christian Polemic. MA thesis, Ben Gurion University.

Schaser, N.J. (2021). The Meaning of the Manger. Israel Bible Weekly, December 20. Retrieved from https://israelbiblecenter.com

Schmitt, J.J. (1991). The Virgin of Israel: Referent and Use of the Phrase in Amos and Jeremiah. The Catholic Biblical Quarterly, 53(3), 365-387.

Smith, S. (2012). The Imahot in the Amidah: A History. Contemporary Jewry, 32, 309-327.

Stone, M.E. (2007). The City in 4 Ezra. Journal of Biblical Literature, 126(2), 402-407.

Theodor, J. & Albeck, C. (1965). Midrash Bereshit Rabba: Critical Edition with Notes and Commentary (3 vols.). Jerusalem: Wahrmann.

Vatican's Pontifical Council for the Pastoral Care of Migrants and Itinerant People (1999). The Shrine: Memory, Presence and Prophecy of the Living God.

Made in the USA
Coppell, TX
04 December 2024

41778781R00077